BOOK
5

WORDLY WISE
3OOO®

Direct Academic Vocabulary Instruction

Fourth Edition

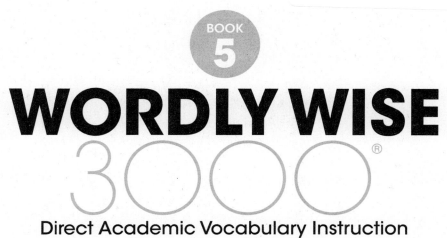

Kenneth Hodkinson • Sandra Adams • Erika Hodkinson

EDUCATORS PUBLISHING SERVICE
Cambridge and Toronto

Editorial team: Carolyn Daniels, Marie Sweetman, Erika Wentworth
Cover Design: Deborah Rodman, Karen Swyers
Interior Design: Deborah Rodman

Vocabulary Extension Illustrations: Chris Murphy

Passage Illustrations for Lessons 3, 8, 16, 18: Q2AMedia

Passage Photograph Credits: Lesson 1: Boris Djuranovic/Fotolia; Lesson 2: Howard Sandler/Fotolia; Lesson 4: Jim Curran/Fotolia; Lesson 5: Masterfile; Lesson 6: Library of Congress Prints and Photographs Division Washington, D.C. 20540 USA; Lesson 7: Thomas Kokta/Masterfile; Lesson 9: John Foxx; Lesson 10: Library of Congress Prints and Photographs Division Washington, D.C. 20540 USA; Lesson 11: Dwight Smith/Fotolia; Lesson 12: Nathalie Speliers Ufermann/Dreamstime; Lesson 13: Unclesam/ Fotolia; Lesson 14: Library of Congress Prints and Photographs Division Washington, D.C. 20540 USA; Lesson 15: Masterfile; Lesson 17: iStockphoto/Thinkstock; Lesson 19: Hemera/Thinkstock; Lesson 20: Martina Berg/Fotolia

Printed in Benton Harbor, MI, in May 2018
ISBN 978-0-8388-7703-6

3 4 5 PPG 21 20 19 18

Contents

Welcome to *Wordly Wise 3000*®

You've been learning words since you were a tiny baby. At first, you learned them only by hearing other people talk. Now that you are a reader, you have another way to learn words.

Obviously, it's important to know what words mean, but lots of times, we think we can get away without knowing some of them as we read. This could cause a problem. Say you are reading the directions for a new game. You know most of the words in the sentence you're reading. Then you stop for a word you don't recognize:

> *Please do not touch the* blegmy *or your score will be lost.*

You ask yourself, "What is a *blegmy?*" At first you think, "Well, it's only one word." But then you think, "What is it that I'm not supposed to touch?" All of a sudden, knowing what that one word means is important!

Clearly, the more words you know, the better your understanding of everything you read. *Wordly Wise 3000* will help you learn a lot of words, but it can't teach you *all* the words you'll ever need. It can, however, help guide your learning of new words on your own.

How Do You Learn What Words Mean?

There are two main ways you learn what words mean: directly and indirectly.

You have to learn some words *directly*. You may study them for a class, look them up in a dictionary or glossary, or ask someone what they mean. You also learn word meanings *indirectly* by hearing and reading the words. In fact, the more you listen and read, the more words you'll learn. Reading books, magazines, and online can help build your vocabulary.

At school, you learn a lot of words directly. If you're using this book, you are learning words directly. You are reading the words, learning what they mean, and studying them. Then you are practicing them as you do the activities. Finally, you might even use them in your own writing or conversations. There is an old saying: "Use a word three times and it's yours." Three times might not be enough, of course, but the idea is right. The more you practice using a word, the better you understand it.

What Is "School Language"?

School language—or school words—are the words you find in the books you read, from novels to textbooks, and on tests. You read them online as you look up information. Your teacher uses these words to explain an important concept about math or reading. Some have to do with a particular topic, such as the building of the Great Pyramid in Egypt. Others are words for tasks you are being asked to do, such as *summarize*. These words are different from the kinds of words you use when you're hanging out with your friends or talking casually with your family. That's why you often need to study such words directly. In this book, these important words are underlined to help you focus on them.

Wordly Wise 3000 is designed to teach you some of the words you need to do well in school and on tests—and later on in your jobs. It will also help you learn how to learn more words. Remember, there is no single thing that will help you understand what you read as much as knowing word meanings will.

How Do You Figure Out Word Meanings?

What should you do when you come to a word and you think you don't know what it means?

Say It

First, say it to yourself. Maybe once you do this, it will sound like a word you *do* know. Sometimes you know a word in your head without knowing what it looks like in print. So if you match up what you know and what you read—you have the word!

Use Context

If this doesn't work, take the next step: look at the context of the word— the other words and sentences around it. Sometimes these can give you a clue to the word's meaning. Here's an example:

> *Mr. Huerta had great respect for his* opponent.

Say that you don't know what *opponent* means. Does Mr. Huerta have respect for his teacher? His mother? Then you read on:

The two players sat across from each other in the warm room. The chessboard was between them. Both looked as if they were concentrating very hard.

Now you see that Mr. Huerta is taking part in a chess game. You know that in a chess game, one person plays another. So his *opponent* must be the person he is playing against. You reread the sentence using that meaning. Yes, that works. In this sentence, *opponent* means "someone you play against, or compete with."

Use Word Parts

If the context doesn't help, look at the parts of the word. Does it have any prefixes you know? How about suffixes? Or roots? These can help you figure out what it means. Look at this sentence:

Shania had the misfortune *to hurt her arm right before the swim meet.*

If you don't know the meaning of *misfortune*, try looking at parts of the word. You might know that *fortune* means "luck." Maybe *mis-* is a prefix. You could look it up, or maybe you remember its meaning from studying prefixes in school. The prefix *mis-* means a few different things, but one of them is "bad." You try it out and reread the sentence using that meaning. It would certainly be bad luck, or a *misfortune,* to hurt your arm before a swim meet.

Look It Up

If saying the word or using context and word parts don't work, you can look it up in a dictionary—either a book or online reference—or a glossary.

Nobody knows the meaning of every word, but good readers know how to use these strategies to figure out words they don't know. Get into the habit of using them as you read, and you may be surprised at how automatic it becomes!

How Well Do You Know a Word?

It's important to know many words and to keep on learning more. But it's also important to know them well. In fact, some experts say that there are four levels of knowing a word:

1. I never saw/heard it before.
2. I've heard/seen it, but I don't know what it means.
3. I think it has something to do with…
4. I know it.*

Just because you can read a word and have memorized its definition, it doesn't mean that you know that word well. You want to know it so well that you know when to use it and when to use another word instead. One way to help deepen your knowledge of a word is to use a graphic organizer like the one below that tells about the word *portion*.

Concept of Definition Map

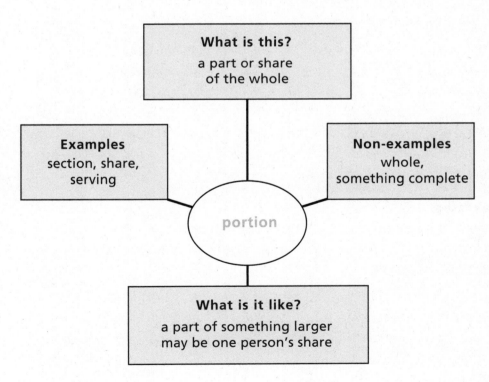

If you can fill in all the parts of this graphic organizer, you are well on your way to really knowing the word *portion*.

*Dale, E., & O'Rourke, J. (1986). *Vocabulary Building*. Columbus, OH: Zaner-Bloser.

Study the definitions of the words. Then do the exercises that follow.

accustom
ə kus´ təm

v. To make familiar.
Every fall the students **accustom** themselves to the new schedule.

accustomed *adj.* 1. Usual.
We sat in our **accustomed** places.

2. Used to.
My eyes soon became **accustomed** to the dark.

Talk to your partner about something at school you had to become accustomed to.

alert
ə lʉrt´

adj. Watchful; wide-awake.
The shortstop was not **alert** and missed the catch.

v. To warn to be ready.
A sign **alerted** drivers to the flooded road ahead.

n. A warning signal.
Because of the forest fires, the nearby towns have a fire **alert.**

assign
ə sīn´

v. 1. To select for a position or for what has to be done.
For this year's basketball team, the coach **assigned** me to play as a forward.

2. To give out, as a piece of work to be done.
Our science teacher usually **assigns** two chapters a week as homework.

assignment *n.* Whatever is given out as work to be done.
What was the **assignment** for tomorrow's history class?

Tell your partner about the teacher you were assigned to last year.

budge
buj

v. To move or shift.
The old metal trunk was so heavy we could not **budge** it.

burly
bʉr´ le

adj. Big and strongly built.
Most football players are quite **burly.**

companion
kəm pan´ yən

n. One who spends time with or does things with another.
My grandmother was always an interesting **companion** when we went to the city for the day.

compatible kəm pat´ ə bəl	*adj.* Getting along well together. Julie and I didn't mind sharing a room, because we were so **compatible**.
concept kän´ sept	*n.* A general idea or thought about something. For our project, we started with the **concept** of helping our community. . . . . *Discuss with your partner your concept of the perfect day.*
distract di strakt´	*v.* To draw one's thoughts or attention away from the subject at hand. The police sirens **distracted** me, so I didn't hear what you said. **distraction** *n.* Something that draws one's thoughts or attention away. I do my homework during study period when there are no **distractions**. . . . . *Talk to your partner about how to handle distractions when you need to do schoolwork.*
jostle jas´ əl	*v.* To push or shove. I dropped my phone when someone in the crowd **jostled** me.
obedient ō be´ dē ənt	*adj.* Doing what one is asked or told. When giving orders, my mother expects all of us to be **obedient**. **obedience** *n.* The state or condition of doing what one is told. We are trying to teach **obedience** to our new puppy. . . . . *Tell your partner what might happen if you are not obedient in school.*
obstacle äb´ stə kəl	*n.* Something that prevents one from moving forward. The **obstacle** holding up traffic was a tree blown over by last night's storm.
patient pā´ shənt	*adj.* Willing to wait without complaining. The audience was very **patient** even though the show started thirty minutes late. *n.* A person in a doctor's care. The **patients** in this part of the hospital are recovering from operations. **patience** *n.* A willingness to wait for someone or something without complaining. Having to stand in line for an hour to buy tickets really tested my **patience**. . . . . *Tell your partner why it's important to have patience.*
pedestrian pə des´ trē ən	*n.* A person who is walking; someone traveling on foot. **Pedestrians** should use the crosswalk to avoid accidents.

retire
rē tīr´

v. 1. To stop working because one has reached a certain age.
My grandfather wishes he could quit his job and **retire,** but he needs to work a few more years.

2. To go to bed.
I was not feeling well, so I **retired** early.

retirement *n.* The state of no longer working.
Uncle Eli regularly saved money for his **retirement.**

Discuss with your partner what time you need to retire each night so you get enough rest.

1A Finding Meanings

Choose two phrases to form a sentence that correctly uses a word from Word List 1. Then write the sentence.

1. (a) become familiar with it.

    (b) do it carefully.

    (c) To accustom oneself to something is to

    (d) To distract oneself by doing something is to

    _____

    _____

2. (a) is under a doctor's care.

    (b) A patient is a person who

    (c) A companion is one who

    (d) gives hope to others.

    _____

    _____

3. (a) An assignment is

    (b) A concept is

    (c) a general idea about something.

    (d) something that stands in the way.

    _____

    _____

4. (a) has traveled a lot.

    (b) A pedestrian is someone who

    (c) spends time with another person.

    (d) A companion is someone who

    _____

    _____

5. (a) An alert is
   (b) a meeting arranged
       in advance.
   (c) work given out to be done.
   (d) An assignment is

   _____

   _____

6. (a) Patience is
   (b) Obedience is
   (c) help and support given to another.
   (d) the willingness to wait without
       complaining.

   _____

   _____

7. (a) is big and strong.
   (b) gets along with others.
   (c) An alert person is one who
   (d) A burly person is one who

   _____

   _____

8. (a) Obedience is
   (b) Retirement is
   (c) a drawing away of one's attention.
   (d) a time when one no longer works.

   _____

   _____

9. (a) To jostle someone is
   (b) to warn the person of danger.
   (c) To distract someone is
   (d) to bump up against that person.

   _____

   _____

10. (a) go to bed.
    (b) To budge is to
    (c) To retire is to
    (d) do as one is told.

   _____

   _____

accustom

alert

assign

budge

burly

companion

compatible

concept

distract

jostle

obedient

obstacle

patient

pedestrian

retire

Just the Right Word

Replace each phrase in bold with a single word (or form of the word) from the word list.

1. They expected their children to be **willing to do as they were told.**

2. My grandparents plan to travel to other countries when they **give up working at their jobs.**

3. They refused to **make the slightest move** even though we pleaded with them to step aside.

4. If you and your roommate are not **able to get along,** you should split up.

5. Elido sounded the **signal that warned of danger** when he saw smoke.

6. We made our way around the **objects that were blocking our way** and continued on our journey.

7. A buzzing mosquito can be a **thing that draws your attention away** when you are trying to read.

8. The camp director **gave out jobs and sent** us to the kitchen crew.

9. You see very few **people out walking** this early in the morning.

10. My sister is more **willing to accept delays without complaining** than I am.

Applying Meanings

Circle the letter or letters next to each correct answer. There may be more than one correct answer.

1. Which of the following could be an **obstacle?**
   (a) lack of money
   (b) a fallen tree
   (c) poor eyesight
   (d) a pleasant voice

2. In which of the following places would a **pedestrian** be?
   (a) on the sidewalk
   (b) inside a car
   (c) in a favorite armchair
   (d) on a plane

3. Which of the following could **distract** someone?
   (a) loud noises
   (b) whispering
   (c) dreams
   (d) the radio

4. Which of the following usually learn **obedience?**
   (a) dogs
   (b) soldiers
   (c) raccoons
   (d) children

5. Which of the following must be **alert?**
   (a) a watchman
   (b) a babysitter
   (c) a driver
   (d) a pilot

6. Which of the following would you expect to be **compatible?**
   (a) friends
   (b) partners
   (c) enemies
   (d) teammates

7. Which of the following could be **assigned?**
   (a) jobs
   (b) rooms
   (c) seats
   (d) birthdays

8. Which of the following might make a good **companion?**
   (a) a dog
   (b) a canoe
   (c) a friend
   (d) a meal

accustom

alert

assign

budge

burly

companion

compatible

concept

distract

jostle

obedient

obstacle

patient

pedestrian

retire

1D Word Study: Synonyms and Antonyms

Circle the two synonyms in each group of four words.

Synonyms are words that have the same or similar meanings. *Vanish* and *disappear* are synonyms. Both words have to do with passing out of sight.

1. budge	warn	shift	accustom
2. distract	return	retire	quit
3. concept	barrier	venture	obstacle
4. warning	light	sound	alert
5. jostle	shove	assign	choose

Circle the two antonyms in each group of four words.

Antonyms are words that have opposite or nearly opposite meanings. *Rise* and *fall* are antonyms. Both words have to do with movement, but in different directions.

6. alert	drowsy	compatible	patient
7. familiar	slight	alert	burly
8. precious	dreary	unfamiliar	accustomed
9. unsteady	obedient	defiant	watchful
10. assign	retire	jostle	arise

Friends for Life

The **concept** that trained dogs could act as eyes for visually disabled people developed at the beginning of the twentieth century in Germany at a remarkable school. The pupils were not humans; they were dogs who learned how to lead people who were blind. The notion caught on quickly. Guide dogs, or Seeing Eye dogs as they are also known, began to be trained in many countries. They are now a familiar sight. These **patient** and loyal animals lead their **companions** everywhere they go. They enable their owners to make their way in the world almost as well as sighted persons.

Not every breed of dog has the exceptional qualities that make a good guide. Seeing Eye dogs must be **alert** at all times, so dogs that are easily **distracted** are not suitable candidates for this exacting job. Labrador retrievers, German shepherds, and boxers make excellent guides. They are smart and easy to train, and they usually get along with people. During its training, the dog is escorted to many kinds of busy places. This is to get it **accustomed** to anything that might occur. A dog is trained in large stores, noisy airports, and crowded restaurants. It rides on buses and in taxis. It is pushed and poked. It learns to disregard anything that might cause its attention to wander.

The Seeing Eye dog is responsible for steering its owner with the utmost care past any **obstacles.** On busy sidewalks, the dog must skillfully weave its way around other **pedestrians.** This is to ensure that its owner doesn't get **jostled.** A guide dog is trained to come to a stop just before it reaches a curb; this is the way it informs its owner to take a step up or down. A guide dog learns to be **obedient,** of course. But it is also taught that there may be situations where it must disobey. For example, say its owner tells it to cross a street when a car is coming. It won't **budge** until it determines that it is safe to cross. While it is being trained, a guide dog is never punished for making a mistake; on the contrary, it is encouraged to do better by being rewarded with praise.

When the training is complete, a guide dog is **assigned** to its new owner. The two of them need to be **compatible;** they will be together for a long time. The size, weight, and nature of both are taken into consideration. A **burly** person might be more comfortable with a large dog. A person who

accustom
alert
assign
budge
burly
companion
compatible
concept
distract
jostle
obedient
obstacle
patient
pedestrian
retire

spends most of the day inside probably will not want to be matched with an energetic dog that needs plenty of exercise. From the beginning, a strong connection needs to form between the dog and the owner.

The Seeing Eye headquarters are located in Morristown, New Jersey. The Seeing Eye is the oldest school for guide dogs in the United States. Every year several hundred people who are blind spend a month there. They learn how to communicate with the dogs they have been matched with. Usually a guide dog stays with its owner for about ten years before it **retires.** Then it may go live with friends of the owner. The dog may remain with them as a traditional family pet for the remainder of its life.

▶ **Answer each of the following questions with a sentence. If a question does not contain a vocabulary word from the lesson's word list, use one in your answer. Use each word only once.**

1. What was the **concept** behind the Seeing Eye dog movement?

   _____

   _____

2. When does the relationship between guide dog and owner officially begin?

   _____

   _____

3. What sort of dog might a **burly** person be matched up with?

   _____

   _____

4. Why do you think a powerful dog would not be matched with someone who is not very strong?

   _____

   _____

5. Where are you most likely to see **pedestrians?**

   _____

   _____

6. **Obedience** is important in dogs kept as pets. Why is this not always true of guide dogs?

_____

_____

7. Why is pushing and poking a guide dog necessary during its training?

_____

_____

8. What is the meaning of **alert** as it is used in the passage?

_____

_____

9. How will a guide dog respond if it is ordered to cross a street with heavy traffic?

_____

_____

10. Why are guide dogs unlikely to get excited when another dog approaches?

_____

_____

11. What is the meaning of **patient** as it is used in the passage?

_____

_____

12. Name three **obstacles** that a guide dog might have to deal with on the street.

_____

_____

13. Why do guide dogs need to keep a watchful eye on other people in crowded places?

_____

_____

| accustom |
| alert |
| assign |
| budge |
| burly |
| companion |
| compatible |
| concept |
| distract |
| jostle |
| obedient |
| obstacle |
| patient |
| pedestrian |
| retire |

14. What is the meaning of **retires** as it is used in the passage?

_____

_____

15. Why would it be somewhat surprising to see a guide dog without its owner?

_____

_____

Fun & Fascinating FACTS

- **Alert** comes from the Italian *all'erta,* which at one time meant "acting as a lookout on a watchtower." The person in the watchtower had to be *alert* (adjective, meaning "watchful"); the person would *alert* the others in the event of danger (verb, meaning "to warn") by sounding the alert (noun, meaning "warning signal"). To be *on the alert* means "to be watchful and ready."

- If you live with or travel with a **companion,** you will probably eat your meals together. This was the case with the Romans, too. The word comes from the Latin prefix *com-,* which means "with," and the word *panis,* which is Latin for "bread." To the Romans, a *companion* was a person with whom one shared a meal, of which bread was one of the main items.

- A **pedestrian** is a person who gets around on foot. A *pedal* is a lever operated by the foot. A *quadruped* is a creature with four feet, while a *centipede* supposedly has 100 feet (it actually has about seventy). All these words come from the Latin *ped-,* whose meaning you can probably guess.

concept

noun An idea that shows how something is or how it should work.

Academic Context

In art, you will practice the **concept** of using different shades of color to produce different effects.

Word Family

conception (noun)
conceptual (adjective)

Discussion & Writing Prompt

Think about your science class. Describe a **concept** you learned about recently.

2 min.	3 min.
1. Turn and talk to your partner or group.	2. Write 2–4 sentences.
Use this space to take notes or draw your ideas.	Be ready to share what you have written.

Word List

Study the definitions of the words. Then do the exercises that follow.

aroma
ə rō´ mə

n. A smell or odor, especially a pleasant one.
The **aroma** of hot buttered popcorn made our mouths water.

beverage
bev´ ər ij

n. A liquid used as a drink.
When we ordered our **beverages,** I chose lemonade.

bland
bland

adj. 1. Lacking a strong flavor.
I don't really like **bland** foods, so I always have a bottle of hot sauce with me.

2. Not irritating, exciting, or disturbing.
The doctor's **bland** manner soon calmed the crying child.

 Demonstrate for your partner how to speak in a very bland way.

brittle
brit´ l

adj. Easily broken; not flexible.
Candy canes are **brittle** and should be handled with care.

cluster
klus´ tər

n. A number of similar things grouped together.
Clusters of brightly colored flowers grew along the side of the road.

v. To gather or come together in a group.
The children **clustered** around the storyteller.

 Work with your partner to cluster all the books on your table or desk in one place.

combine
kəm bīn´

v. To join or bring together.
We **combine** oil and vinegar to make the salad dressing.

combination *n.* A joining or bringing together.
Our team's victory resulted from a **combination** of hard work and good luck.

consume
kən sōōm´

v. 1. To use up.
Piano practice **consumes** all of Alex's free time.

2. To eat or drink.
A horse **consumes** fifty pounds of hay a day.

3. To do away with or destroy.
The forest fire **consumed** over two thousand acres in Oregon.

 Tell your partner about something that consumes your time after school.

crave
krāv

v. To have a strong desire for.
When he was a teenager, Abraham Lincoln **craved** knowledge so much that he would walk miles to borrow a book he had not read.

craving *n.* A strong desire.
After the hike, we all had a **craving** for lots of cool water.

cultivate
kul´ ti vāt

v. 1. To prepare land for the growing of crops.
Before the spring planting, farmers **cultivate** the soil.

2. To grow or to help to grow.
Ana **cultivates** tomatoes every year in her garden.

3. To encourage development by attention or study.
Parents can **cultivate** a love of nature in their children by taking them on hikes in the country.

Discuss with your partner how you could cultivate in your friends an interest in a sport you love.

equivalent
ē kwiv´ ə lənt

adj. Equal to.
Although the decimal 0.5 and the fraction $\frac{1}{2}$ appear to be different, they are **equivalent** amounts.

n. That which is equal to.
One year of a dog's life is the **equivalent** of seven human years.

Tell your partner what number is equivalent to one dozen.

export
ek spôrt´

v. To send goods to another country for sale.
Colombia **exports** coffee to countries all over the world.

n. (eks´ port) Something exported.
Grain is an important **export** of the United States.

extract
ek strakt´

v. 1. To remove or take out.
Dr. Bogasian will **extract** my wisdom tooth next week.

2. To obtain with an effort.
I **extracted** a promise from them to leave us alone.

n. (eks´ trackt) Something removed or taken out.
Vanilla **extract** comes from the seedpods of vanilla plants.

Try to extract a secret from your partner.

introduce
in trə dōōs´

v. 1. To cause to know; to make known by name.
Let me **introduce** you to my new friend, Manoj.

2. To bring to the attention of, especially for the first time.
Our friends in Hawaii **introduced** us to scuba diving.

3. To bring into use.
The invention of the airplane **introduced** a new way of traveling.

introduction *n.* (in trə duk´ shən) 1. Something spoken or written before the main part.
We read the **introduction** before going on to the rest of the book.

2. The act of being made known by name.
After my **introduction** to the others in the room, I relaxed and enjoyed the party.

Discuss with your partner how cell phones have introduced many ways to share photos.

purchase
pʉr´ chəs

v. To buy.
My older brother is saving money to **purchase** a used car so he can get to his job more easily.

n. 1. Something that is bought.
My aunt came over to give us her **purchases** from the market for Sunday dinner.

2. The act of buying.
I looked at and rode several bicycles before I made a **purchase.**

tropical
träp´ i kəl

adj. 1. Of, from, or similar to the regions near the equator.
Ecuador, which lies on the equator, is a **tropical** country.

2. Hot and moist.
In Miami, we have **tropical** weather even in the winter months.

Using Words in Context

Read the following sentences. If the word in bold is used correctly, write C on the line. If the word is used incorrectly, write I on the line.

1. (a) The **aroma** can be paddled by one person. _____
   (b) The **aroma** of buttered popcorn is the best part of going to the movie theater. _____
   (c) When we entered the restaurant, the **aroma** of freshly baked bread greeted us. _____
   (d) The band played an **aroma** that I'd heard many times before. _____

2. (a) Maria pulled the **cluster** over herself and went to sleep. _____
   (b) The grapes grow in **clusters** and are now ready to be picked. _____
   (c) Penguins **cluster** in large numbers as a way to stay warm. _____
   (d) We turned on the **cluster** to fill the sink with water. _____

3. (a) Are shoes one of your **purchases?** _____
   (b) Alya **purchased** and hugged her mom before school. _____
   (c) The climbers **purchased** their way up the precipice. _____
   (d) The farmers **purchased** new tractors for the fields. _____

4. (a) Playing the video game was **consuming** too much of my time. _____
   (b) A large python is able to **consume** an entire deer, horns and all. _____
   (c) The fire quickly **consumed** the log cabin, but luckily no one was inside. _____
   (d) I **consume** that you will be at school tomorrow. _____

5. (a) The book's **introduction** tells why the book was written. _____
   (b) Paper is **introduced** in bundles at the store. _____
   (c) We **introduced** the soup with fresh basil and garlic. _____
   (d) Rico was **introduced** to archery when he was five years old. _____

6. (a) The land in Pecos is too rocky to be **cultivated.** _____
   (b) The tomato was first **cultivated** in Central America by the Aztecs. _____
   (c) We believe that farmland in ancient Rome was first **cultivated** in the year 625 BCE. _____
   (d) The two best friends **cultivated** a movie on the couch. _____

aroma
beverage
bland
brittle
cluster
combine
consume
crave
cultivate
equivalent
export
extract
introduce
purchase
tropical

7. (a) Mercedes complains that her dad's food is too **bland.** _____
   (b) Spike prefers **bland** music when he's falling asleep. _____
   (c) The recipe said to **bland** the butter and eggs in the bowl. _____
   (d) Viola's **bland** manner hid the fact that she had a bad temper. _____

8. (a) The **combination** of oxygen and hydrogen makes water. _____
   (b) We tried to **combine** the air, but it was too stinky. _____
   (c) My favorite kind of book **combines** mystery with comedy. _____
   (d) We were **combined** to stay away from the candy store by our
       parents. _____

9. (a) Tadita was **extracted** to hear her aunt was coming to visit. _____
   (b) After the juice is **extracted**, the rest of the orange is thrown away. _____
   (c) The drill **extracted** the oil from the earth. _____
   (d) It was the climate that first **extracted** his family to southern
       California. _____

10. (a) Frigid temperatures are **tropical** of Alaskan winters. _____
    (b) You don't expect to see polar bears in a **tropical** country. _____
    (c) The room was so hot and humid, it felt almost **tropical.** _____
    (d) It was **tropical** of Sai to lose his backpack. _____

2B Making Connections

Circle the letter next to each correct answer. There may be more than one correct answer.

1. Which word or words go with *thirsty?*
   (a) aroma   (b) cluster   (c) beverage   (d) brittle

2. Which word or words go with *break?*
   (a) tropical   (b) bland   (c) fragile   (d) brittle

3. Which word or words go with *want very much?*
   (a) consume   (b) desire   (c) cluster   (d) crave

4. Which word or words go with *equal?*
   (a) equipment   (b) equivalent   (c) combination   (d) introduction

5. Which word or words go with *sell to another country?*
   (a) exceed   (b) exclaim   (c) export   (d) extract

6. Which word or words go with *dull?*
   (a) bland   (b) dreary   (c) brittle   (d) drab

7. Which word or words go with *get?*
   (a) purchase   (b) introduce   (c) cluster   (d) obtain

8. Which word or words go with *eat?*
   (a) purchase   (b) consume   (c) digest   (d) combine

9. Which word or words go with *grow?*
   (a) mature   (b) elevate   (c) develop   (d) cultivate

10. Which word or words go with *remove?*
    (a) exceed   (b) extract   (c) expose   (d) exclaim

aroma
beverage
bland
brittle
cluster
combine
consume
crave
cultivate
equivalent
export
extract
introduce
purchase
tropical

Determining Meanings

Circle the letter next to each answer choice that correctly completes the sentence. There may be more than one correct answer.

1. The **beverage**
   (a) was made from milk and strawberries.
   (b) of sand got all over the floor.
   (c) spun out of control when it hit a rock.
   (d) came with lunch in the cafeteria.

2. **Clusters**
   (a) of smoke rose from the chimney.
   (b) of rain came suddenly, so we ran inside.
   (c) of nuts were found in the tree near the squirrel's nest.
   (d) of medals were worn proudly by the Olympians.

3. A **craving**
   (a) can be very strong and powerful.
   (b) for salty foods can be satisfied with pretzels.
   (c) broke, causing the bridge to collapse.
   (d) was included in Nany's birthday present.

4. The **introduction**
   (a) of the airplane made long-distance travel much faster.
   (b) at the beginning of the book was boring.
   (c) in the engine needs gasoline.
   (d) of the new principal took place in the gym.

5. A **tropical**
   (a) island usually has beaches and palm trees.
   (b) breeze caressed us as we sat in the sun.
   (c) friend is one you can rely on.
   (d) mistake is one that could have been easily avoided.

6. We **exported**
   (a) grain to many different countries.
   (b) ourselves if we didn't listen to others.
   (c) items only to places we trusted.
   (d) gifts with each other that we made ourselves.

7. A **combination** of
   (a) leftovers was in one big container for Marisela's lunch.
   (b) the flag was at the top of the flagpole.
   (c) friends and basketball makes for a great afternoon.
   (d) sleeping should be in bed.

8. A **bland**
   (a) was missing from the bookshelf.
   (b) textbook can make class boring.
   (c) food like mashed potatoes can still be delicious.
   (d) is easily mistaken for the real thing.

2D Completing Sentences

Complete the sentences to demonstrate your knowledge of the words in bold.

aroma
beverage
bland
brittle
cluster
combine
consume
crave
cultivate
equivalent
export
extract
introduce
purchase
tropical

1. An example of a **brittle** food is

   _____.

2. If you **combine** black and white, you make the color

   _____.

3. If two things are **equivalent,** that means they are

   _____.

4. An example of something that cannot be **purchased** is

   _____.

5. My favorite food to **consume** is

   _____.

6. If I were visiting a **tropical** country, I would

   _____.

7. I **introduce** myself by saying

   _____.

8. The one thing I **crave** more than anything is

   _____.

9. If my family owned a lot of land, I would **cultivate**

_____ .

10. My favorite **beverage** is

_____ .

2E   Vocabulary in Context
Read the passage.

When Money Grows on Trees

Do you wish that chocolate grew on trees? Well, it does. The trees are cocoa trees that grow in **tropical** countries that are located both north and south of the equator. Of course, you wouldn't recognize the little pale-colored and bitter-tasting beans of the cocoa tree as chocolate. But those beans are the raw material and the main ingredient from which delicious chocolate bars are made.

Cocoa trees were originally **cultivated** in Central and South America. They are now grown in many other parts of the world, including West Africa, the Caribbean, and southern Asia. They thrive in areas with a year-round temperature of around eighty degrees and an annual rainfall of eighty inches or more. However, the young trees need protection from direct sunlight. Banana plants, which are considerably taller, are often interspersed between the rows of cocoa trees to provide the shade these trees need.

Pods as big as footballs grow from the branches and trunks of the cocoa trees. Inside each pod is a **cluster** of twenty to forty cocoa beans. Each bean is located inside its own thin shell. Workers cut the pods from the trees manually and split them open to remove the beans. The beans are then separated and stored in boxes for about a week. When the beans are brown and have developed a slight chocolate **aroma,** they are ready for the next phase—to be dried. After the drying is completed, the beans are put in sacks; these are then **exported** to other countries through a worldwide distribution network.

Now they are ready to be manufactured into chocolate. First, the beans are roasted. This makes the shells **brittle** and easy to separate from the beans. Next the beans are ground into a paste that contains a lot of fat. That fat is called cocoa butter. The cocoa butter is **extracted** from the beans.

What remains is the cocoa powder, which is utilized in the making of chocolate cakes, cookies, and puddings. **Combining** the cocoa powder with cocoa butter, sugar, and dried milk makes the soft, sweet chocolate in candy.

The Spanish explorers who traveled through Central and South America in the 1500s were the first to **introduce** chocolate into Europe. The Aztecs, who lived in what is now Mexico, ground up cocoa beans and made the paste into a cold **beverage.** They must have considered it **bland;** they mixed it with chili peppers and other fiery spices to give it more flavor. Not surprisingly, the name "chocolate" comes from an Aztec word meaning "bitter drink." Montezuma, the Aztec king, appears to have had a **craving** for it. According to Aztec legends, he **consumed** up to fifty cups of chocolate a day!

The Aztecs also utilized cocoa beans as money. A rabbit cost ten beans, while an enslaved person could be **purchased** for a hundred. Sadly, that would have made the value of a human being **equivalent** to ten rabbits. This may seem surprising, but here is something else to think about: The Aztecs actually lived in a land where money grew on trees.

▶ **Answer each of the following questions with a sentence. If a question does not contain a vocabulary word from the lesson's word list, use one in your answer. Use each word only once.**

√	aroma
√	beverage
√	bland
√	brittle
√	cluster
√	combine
√	consume
√	crave
√	cultivate
	equivalent
√	export
√	extract
√	introduce
√	purchase
√	tropical

1. How can one satisfy a **craving** for chocolate?

_____

_____

2. What are two ways that cocoa is used today?

_____

_____

3. What is the meaning of **cultivated** as it is used in the passage?

_____

_____

4. Why do cocoa trees grow only in **tropical** countries?

_____

_____

5. To which countries are cocoa beans **exported?**

_____

_____

6. In addition to using cocoa beans for a drink, in what other way did the Aztecs use them?

_____

_____

7. How is chocolate candy made?

_____

_____

8. What would you find if you split open a pod of the cocoa tree?

_____

_____

9. How do workers know when the cocoa beans are ready to be dried?

_____

_____

10. What is the meaning of **consumed** as it is used in the passage?

_____

_____

11. When can the shells of cocoa beans be removed easily from the beans?

_____

_____

12. How is ground cocoa-bean paste turned into cocoa powder?

_____

_____

13. How and when did Europeans learn about chocolate?

_____

_____

14. What is the meaning of **bland** as it is used in the passage?

_____

_____

15. Why could an Aztec receive five rabbits in exchange for fifty cocoa beans?

_____

_____

aroma
beverage
bland
brittle
cluster
combine
consume
crave
cultivate
equivalent
export
extract
introduce
purchase
tropical

Fun & Fascinating FACTS

- **Aroma** once meant "a spice." Spices have strong and pleasant smells, and in time the meaning of the word changed. An aroma became the pleasant smell of the spice rather than the spice itself. Later the word came to mean any smell, but especially one that is pleasant.

- The word **export** is formed from the Latin prefix *ex-*, meaning "out," and the Latin root *port,* meaning "carry." Goods being *exported* are *carried* by boat or plane *out* of the country. The antonym of *export* is *import.* To *import* goods is to bring them *into* a country. (The United States *imports* many cars from Japan.)

- The Latin *tractus* means "drawn" or "pulled" and forms the root of several English words. A *tractor* is a vehicle used to pull farm machinery. A *protracted* explanation is one that is drawn out and goes on too long. This root joins with the Latin prefix *ex-*, meaning "out," to form the word **extract.**

- The adjective **tropical** is formed from the word *tropic.* The Tropic of Cancer and the Tropic of Capricorn are two imaginary lines going around the earth, north and south of the equator. They are three thousand miles apart, and the area of the world between them is called the tropics. Most of Africa and Central and South America and parts of Asia are in the tropics.

extract

verb To remove; to take out.

noun Something that has been removed or taken out.

Word Family

extracted (verb)
extraction (noun)

Context Clues

These sentences give clues to the meaning of **extracted.**

> *The dentist **extracted** Stephanie's painful tooth.*
> *Marcus **extracted** the coins from his pocket to pay for the orange juice.*

Discussion & Writing Prompt

If your baseball rolled under a thorny bush, how would you **extract** it?

2 min.	**3 min.**
1. Turn and talk to your partner or group.	2. Write 2–4 sentences.
Use this space to take notes or draw your ideas.	Be ready to share what you have written.

Study the definitions of the words. Then do the exercises that follow.

ancestor
an´ ses tər

n. 1. A person from whom one is descended.
My **ancestors** came from Congo.

2. An early kind of animal from which later ones have developed; a forerunner.
The dog-sized mesohippus is the **ancestor** of the modern horse.

carnivore
kär´ ni vôr

n. A flesh-eating animal.
Carnivores have sharp, pointed teeth that enable them to tear the meat they eat.

carnivorous *adj.* (kär niv´ ər əs) Flesh-eating.
Although dogs are **carnivorous,** they will often eat other foods besides meat.

comprehend
käm prē hend´

v. To understand.
If you don't **comprehend** the question, I will word it differently.

comprehension *n.* The act of understanding; the ability to understand.
Pawel cannot speak Spanish very well, but his **comprehension** is quite good.

Show your partner what you look like if you don't comprehend something.

duration
door ā´ shən

n. The time during which something lasts or continues.
We stayed in our house for the **duration** of the heavy rainstorm.

evident
ev´ ə dənt

adj. Easy to see and understand; obvious, clear.
It is **evident** from your manner that you are not happy to see me.

Make a face at your partner that makes your feelings evident, and then ask your partner to guess your feelings.

extinct
ek stiŋkt´

adj. 1. No longer existing or living.
The giant woolly mammoth went **extinct** about ten thousand years ago.

2. No longer active.
Mount Saint Helens was believed to be an **extinct** volcano until it suddenly became active in 1980.

ferocious
fə rō´ shəs

adj. Savage; fierce.
Doberman pinschers make **ferocious** guard dogs.

ferocity *n.* (fə räs´ ə tē) The state or quality of being fierce.
The **ferocity** of the storm surprised us.

Show your partner what you look like if you act with ferocity.

gigantic
jī gan´ tik

adj. Very large; like a giant in size.
The *Spruce Goose* was a **gigantic** airplane that made only one flight.

obscure
äb skyoor´

v. To cover up or keep from being seen.
Clouds **obscured** the moon.

adj. 1. Hard to see; hidden.
The boat was an **obscure** shape in the mist.

2. Not easy to understand.
The story was full of **obscure** words like "cauldron" and "phoenix."

Tell your partner what you think is the most obscure thing your teacher has said this week.

option
äp´ shən

n. Choice, or something that is available as a choice.
We had the **option** of practicing soccer during the lunch break or after school.

optional *adj.* Left to choice.
Papi said we had to go to Tia Maria's house for lunch, but staying for dinner was **optional.**

Discuss with your partner whether going to school should be optional.

premature
prē mə choor´

adj. Too early; happening or arriving before the proper time.
Premature babies require special care before they are allowed to leave the hospital.

preserve
prē zʉrv´

v. 1. To save; to keep from harm; to protect.
This law will help **preserve** the old forests in the national parks.

2. To keep from rotting or spoiling.
Steve and Martha **preserve** the peaches from their orchard by canning them.

prey
prā

n. 1. An animal that is hunted for food.
Chickens are the natural **prey** of foxes.

2. One that is helpless or unable to resist attack; a victim.
Be alert when you travel so that you will not be **prey** to thieves.

v. 1. To hunt (animals) for food.
Wolves **prey** on the weakest deer in the herd.

2. To take from or rob using violence or trickery.
The pickpockets **preyed** on people whose arms were full of shopping bags.

Tell your partner how an animal might avoid becoming prey.

puny
pyo͞o′nē

adj. 1. Weak.
Lifting weights can change **puny** muscles into powerful ones.

2. Lacking in size, strength, or power.
My offering of one dollar seemed **puny** compared to what others gave.

survive
sər vīv′

v. 1. To stay alive where there is a chance of dying or being killed.
Only three passengers **survived** the plane crash.

2. To continue living or existing through a threatening situation.
Only two of the eight maple trees in our yard **survived** the hurricane.

survivor *n.* One who stays alive in a situation where others die.
Survivors of the shipwreck floated on life rafts until the helicopter could pick them up.

Talk to your partner about how you would survive if you were alone on an island.

Finding Meanings

Choose two phrases to form a sentence that correctly uses a word from Word List 3. Then write the sentence.

1. (a) it is easy to see.
   (b) If something is evident,
   (c) If something is premature,
   (d) it has lasted for a long time.

_____

_____

2. (a) from whom one is descended.   (c) An ancestor is someone
   (b) who does not eat meat.   (d) A survivor is someone

   _____

   _____

3. (a) To prey on wildlife is to   (c) keep it from harm.
   (b) To preserve wildlife is to   (d) have a complete understanding of it.

   _____

   _____

4. (a) A gigantic volcano is one that (c) is no longer active.
   (b) An extinct volcano is one that   (d) is hidden from view.

   _____

   _____

5. (a) is to let it get away.   (c) To prey on something
   (b) To obscure something   (d) is to hunt it for food.

   _____

   _____

6. (a) The comprehension of   (c) the length of time it is delayed.
       something is
   (b) the length of time that it lasts. (d) The duration of something is

   _____

   _____

7. (a) that is very big.   (c) A puny figure is one
   (b) that is well known.   (d) A gigantic figure is one

   _____

   _____

8. (a) is one that has not died out.   (c) A practice that is optional
   (b) is one that seems strange.   (d) A practice that survives

   _____

   _____

9. (a) one that leaves nothing out.   (c) An obscure report is
   (b) A premature report is   (d) one that is hard to understand.

   _____

   _____

10. (a) A ferocious creature is   (c) An extinct creature is
    (b) one that has died out.   (d) one that eats only meat.

   _____

   _____

3B Just the Right Word

Replace each phrase in bold with a single word (or form of the word) from the word list.

ancestor
carnivore
comprehend
duration
evident
extinct
ferocious
gigantic
obscure
option
premature
preserve
prey
puny
survive

1. The house was **hidden from view** by a thick hedge.

2. My two-horsepower engine is **lacking in power** compared to the fifty-horsepower one in your boat.

3. It is **easy to see** from the dishes in the sink that someone has already eaten lunch.

4. The film captures the **fierce behavior** of a mother tiger defending her cubs.

5. The pirate Blackbeard **attacked and robbed the people** on ships in the Caribbean.

6. To announce the holiday schedule now would be **to do so before the time is right.**

7. After the flood, the **people who remained alive** returned to their homes to clean away the mud.

8. Alberto had no other **choice available** but to take the test on Friday, even though he was still sick.

9. We did not stay for the **entire time** of the concert because Madeleine was too tired.

10. Lions and tigers are **animals that eat meat.**

3C Applying Meanings

Circle the letter or letters next to each correct answer. There may be more than one correct answer.

1. Which of the following is **optional** on most bikes?
   (a) brakes
   (b) tires
   (c) basket
   (d) bike lock

2. Which of the following can be **preserved?**
   (a) freedom
   (b) fruit
   (c) letters
   (d) clouds

3. Which of the following can become **extinct?**
   (a) languages
   (b) volcanoes
   (c) plants
   (d) animals

4. Which of the following is an **ancestor?**
   (a) your brother
   (b) your daughter
   (c) your great-grandmother
   (d) your grandson

5. Which of the following are **carnivorous?**
   (a) wolves
   (b) horses
   (c) cows
   (d) bees

6. Which of the following can be **premature?**
   (a) a death
   (b) a holiday
   (c) an announcement
   (d) a baby

7. Which of the following might be **ferocious?**
   (a) a polar bear
   (b) a teddy bear
   (c) a hungry dog
   (d) a hungry baby

8. Which of the following might be hard to **comprehend**?
   (a) a computer game   (c) a foreign language
   (b) a shopping list   (d) a card game

3D   Word Study: Latin Roots

In each space, write the Latin word forming the root of each English word, together with its meaning. Choose from the ten Latin words shown.

Many English words come from Latin roots. The word *liberty,* for example, is formed from the Latin word *liber,* meaning "free."

cultus (plow)   *trahere* (to draw)   *ferox* (fierce)
praematurus (very early) *vivere* (to live)   *carnis* (meat)
durare (to last)   *videre* (to see)
pedester (on foot)   *prehendere* (grasp)

Definition	English Word	Latin Word

1. not fully formed   premature   _____

    Meaning _____

2. to stay alive   survive   _____

    Meaning _____

3. meat-eating   carnivore   _____

    Meaning _____

4. with great savagery ferocious   _____

    Meaning _____

5. one who goes on foot pedestrian   _____

    Meaning _____

6. to till or work the soil cultivate _____

    Meaning _____

ancestor
carnivore
comprehend
duration
evident
extinct
ferocious
gigantic
obscure
option
premature
preserve
prey
puny
survive

7. to draw attention away   distract   _____

   Meaning _____

8. to grasp the meaning of   comprehend   _____

   Meaning _____

9. the time something lasts   duration   _____

   Meaning _____

10. plain to see   evident   _____

   Meaning _____

3E Vocabulary in Context

Read the passage.

The Last Dinosaurs

When people think of dinosaurs, the one that comes to mind most frequently is *Tyrannosaurus rex*. This **gigantic** monster was almost fifty feet in length and weighed five tons. *Tyrannosaurus rex* had curved eight-inch talons on its feet. It also had a huge jaw lined with teeth as long and as sharp as steak knives. It was thought to have been the most terrifying of all the **carnivorous** dinosaurs. Imagine the surprise, then, of some scientists who were digging in eastern Utah in 1992. They found **preserved** in the rock the remains of a dinosaur. Not just any dinosaur, but one that could well have been a match for *Tyrannosaurus rex*.

Named *Utahraptor*, this **ferocious** creature was "only" twenty feet long. But it had twelve-inch hooked claws on each of its hind legs. Unlike *Tyrannosaurus rex*, which had surprisingly short and **puny** forelimbs, *Utahraptor* had large, powerful arms equipped with ten-inch claws. With these it could grasp its **prey** and bring its victim down. Then it could slash with the terrible claws on its hind feet. Flight was not an **option** for an animal being attacked. The *Utahraptor* had sturdy back legs. It could probably outrun any other creature. But a contest between these two powerful creatures of the dinosaur world was not to be. It never took place, for one reason: All of the *Utahraptors* had been dead for fifty million years before *Tyrannosaurus rex* ever appeared.

It is difficult to **comprehend** the vast stretch of time that dinosaurs lived on Earth. They lasted well over a hundred and fifty million years. *Tyrannosaurus rex* was among the last of the dinosaurs; it died out sixty-five million years ago. Human beings have been around for only two or three million years. It will be a long time before we equal the **duration** of the dinosaurs' stay on Earth.

No one knows why these creatures became **extinct.** But it seems **evident** from the record left in Earth's crust that it happened fairly suddenly. We know that a meteorite, a large mass of rock or metal from outer space, once hit Earth. This was in what is now Mexico about sixty-five million years ago. The meteorite made a crater almost two hundred miles across. Dust from such an impact would have **obscured** the light from the sun for many weeks. The result would have been freezing temperatures. Much of Earth's plant life would have died. That would have made it difficult for many animals to **survive.**

However, it would be **premature** to say for certain that this was what brought an end to the dinosaurs; scientists are still studying the subject. Indeed, scientists in China have discovered the bones of *Sinornis*, a feathered dinosaur that perched and flew. This has led some to claim that this creature may be the **ancestor** of today's birds. If this turns out to be true, then it would be possible to say that the dinosaurs never died out at all.

ancestor
carnivore
comprehend
duration
evident
extinct
ferocious
gigantic
obscure
option
premature
preserve
prey
puny
survive

▶ **Answer each of the following questions with a sentence. If a question does not contain a vocabulary word from the lesson's word list, use one in your answer. Use each word only once.**

1. How do scientists know that *Utahraptor* ever lived?

_____

_____

2. What was the **duration** of the age of the dinosaurs?

_____

_____

3. When did the last of the dinosaurs die out?

_____

_____

4. What are some things scientists now **comprehend** about *Utahraptor?*

_____

_____

5. What is the meaning of **prey** as it is used in the passage?

_____

_____

6. How did *Tyrannosaurus rex* compare in size to *Utahraptor?*

_____

_____

7. What is the meaning of **survive** as it is used in the passage?

_____

_____

8. What were the **options** of a creature attacked by *Utahraptor?*

_____

_____

9. Were the forelimbs of *Tyrannosaurus rex* as powerful as those of *Utahraptor?* Why or why not?

_____

_____

10. Why is it **premature** to say for certain what brought an end to the dinosaurs?

_____

_____

11. Did the dinosaurs die out over a long period of time?

_____

_____

12. Why would a meteorite crashing into Earth affect the sunlight?

_____

_____

13. Why do some scientists say a dinosaur may be the **ancestor** of birds?

_____

_____

14. How would you describe the eating habits of _Tyrannosaurus rex_ and _Utahraptor_?

_____

_____

15. Why would other creatures probably try to avoid _Utahraptor_?

_____

_____

ancestor
carnivore
comprehend
duration
evident
extinct
ferocious
gigantic
obscure
option
premature
preserve
prey
puny
survive

Fun & Fascinating FACTS

- A **carnivore** is a meat-eating animal, especially a mammal that hunts for its food. Certain plants that eat insects, such as the Venus flytrap, are also _carnivorous_. The word comes from the Latin _carn_, which means "meat" or "flesh." _Chili con carne_ is a Spanish phrase in which the word _carne_ comes from the same Latin word; the phrase means "chili with meat."

- **Prey** and _pray_ are homophones, words that sound alike but have different meanings and spellings. To pray means "to ask, request, or plead for help, or to offer praise or thanks."

- The Latin phrase _puis ne_ means "born afterward" and was applied to Roman children of noble birth who followed the firstborn. Because Roman titles and property passed to the oldest, the other children, those who were _puis ne_, were considered to be less powerful. The phrase passed into English as our adjective **puny.**

- Things that are hard, such as stone, iron, or bones, are slow to decay or wear away, so they last a long time. The Romans saw how these two qualities, of being hard and lasting a long time, were related. The Latin words _durus_ "hard," and _durare_, "to last a long time" show this connection and form the root of several English words. In addition to **duration,** there is _endure_, which means "to last a long time." In the United States, the separation of church and state is a concept that has _endured_ for more than two centuries. _Durable_ goods are items such as cars and refrigerators that are expected to last a long time.

evident

adjective Easy to see and understand; clear.

Word Family
evidence (noun)
evidently (adverb)

Synonyms and Antonyms
Synonyms: obvious, clear
Antonyms: mysterious, unclear

Discussion & Writing Prompt

*There was **evidence** that an animal had been in our garden. We could see footprints, and our tomatoes were gone.*

After reading these sentences, what do you think **evidence** means?

`2 min.`	`3 min.`
1. Turn and talk to your partner or group.	**2.** Write 2–4 sentences.
Use this space to take notes or draw your ideas.	Be ready to share what you have written.

Study the definitions of the words. Then do the exercises that follow.

accurate
ak´ yər ət

adj. 1. Able to give a correct reading or measurement.
This clock is so **accurate** that it gains less than one second a year.

2. Without mistakes or errors in facts.
In science class we make **accurate** drawings of the plants we study.

accuracy *n.* Correctness, exactness.
I question the **accuracy** of your report because others have described the accident quite differently.

Look around and give your partner an accurate count of the number of people in the room.

approximate
ə präk´ si mət

adj. Not exact, but close enough to be reasonably correct.
The **approximate** weight of the puppy was ten pounds.

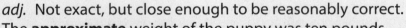

Without looking, tell your partner the approximate number of desks in the room.

course
kôrs

n. 1. The path over which something moves.
The spaceship is now on a **course** for Mars.

2. A way of acting or behaving.
Because it is raining so hard, our best **course** is to wait in the car until the storm ends.

3. A subject or set of subjects to be studied.
The high school science **course** includes several field trips.

Talk to your partner about the best course of action if there is a tornado warning.

depart
dē pärt´

v. To leave; to go away from a place.
The bus for Detroit **departs** at ten o'clock.

departure *n.* The act of leaving.
We were sad after the **departure** of our friends.

despair
də spâr´

v. To lose hope.
When neither the library nor the bookstore had it, I **despaired** of ever finding the book I wanted.

n. A total lack of hope.
The look of **despair** on their faces told me that the situation was worse than I had feared.

| **destination** | *n.* The place to which something or someone is going. |
| des tə nā´ shən | Tell the clerk your **destination** when you buy your ticket. |

| **deteriorate** | *v.* To make or become worse. |
| dē tir´ ē ər āt | The sidewalks in our neighborhood have **deteriorated** because the city has not taken care of them. |

Tell your partner how you would feel if your relationship with your best friend were to deteriorate.

gale	*n.* 1. A very strong wind.
gāl	Last night's **gale** tore several tiles off the roof.
	2. A loud outburst.
	We heard **gales** of laughter coming from the party.

horizon	*n.* The apparent line in the distance where the sky meets the sea or land.
hər ī´ zən	We watched the setting sun sink slowly over the **horizon.**
	horizontal *adj.* (hôr i zänt´ l) Going straight across from side to side.
	The shoeboxes were in a **horizontal** row at the back of the closet.

Show your partner how you can make your hands horizontal.

jubilation	*n.* A feeling or expression of great joy.
jōō bə lā´ shən	There was jubilation among the fans when the team won the championship.
	jubilant *adj.* (jōō´ bə lənt) Very happy.
	My family was **jubilant** when Aunt Fee survived the heart operation.

navigate	*v.* To calculate or direct the movement of a ship or aircraft.
nav´ ə gāt	Sailors **navigate** their ships into port when they need supplies.
	navigation *n.* The science or practice of navigating.
	Mark Twain learned **navigation** during his time on a boat on the Mississippi River.

nostalgia	*n.* A longing for a certain time in the past.
näs tal´ jə	Seeing the photographs of my first dog filled me with **nostalgia.**
	nostalgic *adj.* Having feelings of nostalgia.
	I became **nostalgic** when I heard you playing the song my grandfather used to sing to me.

revive
rē vīv´

v. 1. To make or become strong again.
A short rest will **revive** you.

2. To bring back into use or fashion.
The new musical show **revives** several of our favorite childhood songs.

Talk to your partner about something that might revive you if you were very tired.

sever
sev´ər

v. 1. To break off.
After the argument, the two families **severed** all ties with each other.

2. To cut in two.
Irving accidentally **severed** the garden hose while mowing the lawn.

Tell your partner how you would feel if someone wanted to sever a friendship with you.

voyage
voi´ ij

n. A long journey by sea or in space.
The **voyage** across the Pacific will take three weeks.

v. To make a journey by sea or in space.
Long before Columbus, the Vikings **voyaged** across the Atlantic Ocean to reach North America.

4A Using Words in Context

Read the following sentences. If the word in bold is used correctly, write C on the line. If the word is used incorrectly, write I on the line.

1. (a) I checked the **accuracy** of my watch and found it was one minute slow. ____
   (b) Professional basketball players must be **accurate** with the ball. ____
   (c) As far as we can tell, what he says is **accurate.** ____
   (d) The weather turned **accurate,** so we left early. ____

2. (a) The first **voyage** of the *Titanic* ended in disaster when it hit an iceberg. ____
   (b) Ferdinand Magellan made the first **voyage** around the world in 1521. ____
   (c) The **voyage** reached for the coat at the back of the closet. ____
   (d) We decided to **voyage** by train even though it took longer. ____

3. (a) The **course** the boat is on is toward the first city north of us. ____
   (b) Marvin is taking a **course** on math for extra credit. ____
   (c) Your best **course** if a tornado strikes is to head for the basement. ____
   (d) The recipe calls for a tablespoon of **course** salt. ____

4. (a) There were times when we **despaired** of winning the game. ____
   (b) The song is about the **despair** of someone who is alone. ____
   (c) I was too **despaired** to meet my sister for lunch. ____
   (d) I was **despaired** by the teacher for littering in the lunchroom. ____

5. (a) The **jubilant** look on his face told us he had won. ____
   (b) We heard cries of **jubilation** as we entered the stadium. ____
   (c) We put together a **jubilation** of our favorite songs. ____
   (d) Mansi picked up the **jubilant** and began to play. ____

6. (a) A marble will not roll on a **horizontal** surface. ____
   (b) The **horizon** was purple and pink during the sunset. ____
   (c) I looked through the **horizon,** but it was too foggy to see anything. ____
   (d) The line drawn from left to right in the picture represents the **horizon.** ____

7. (a) When reminded of her old friend, Jacquetta becomes **nostalgic.** ____
   (b) Sal caught **nostalgia** after being bitten by a bug. ____
   (c) Ten thousand dollars is a really **nostalgic** amount of money. ____
   (d) The place I feel most **nostalgic** is my old preschool. ____

8. (a) The batter **severed** the ball into the bleachers. ____
   (b) Luna **severed** the tree limb with one swing of her ax. ____
   (c) If you are banished, you must **sever** all ties with your country. ____
   (d) Mari **severed** the pizza into six equal slices. ____

9. (a) Sheila **revived** her friendship with Santiago by loaning him her
       football. ____
   (b) The space program was **revived** with plans for a trip to Mars. ____
   (c) The music **revives** like nothing but drums. ____
   (d) The smell of garlic **revives** me of spaghetti. ____

10. (a) The school bus **departs** in ten minutes. ____
    (b) The coach's sudden **departure** from the rules shocked everyone. ____
    (c) Natalia and I **departed** but promised to get together again soon. ____
    (d) He softly **departed** on the bed and sighed. ____

Making Connections

Circle the letter next to each correct answer. There may be more than one correct answer.

1. Which word or words go with *wild animal?*
   (a) accurate   (b) ferocious   (c) approximate   (d) horizontal

2. Which word or words go with *not exact?*
   (a) accurate   (b) equivalent   (c) approximate   (d) nostalgic

3. Which word or words go with *travel?*
   (a) depart   (b) deteriorate   (c) destination   (d) voyage

4. Which word or words go with *worsen?*
   (a) deteriorate   (b) navigate   (c) nostalgia   (d) obscure

5. Which word or words go with *weather?*
   (a) forecast   (b) climate   (c) bland   (d) gale

6. Which word or words go with *feelings?*
   (a) accuracy   (b) nostalgia   (c) jubilation   (d) departure

7. Which word or words go with *measuring?*
   (a) departure   (b) accurate   (c) approximate   (d) jubilation

8. Which word or words go with *unhappiness?*
   (a) misery   (b) jubilation   (c) combination (d) despair

9. Which word or words go with *straight?*
   (a) bland   (b) horizontal   (c) nostalgic   (d) evident

10. Which word or words go with *recover?*
    (a) scurry   (b) deprive   (c) deteriorate   (d) revive

accurate
approximate
course
depart
despair
destination
deteriorate
gale
horizon
jubilation
navigate
nostalgia
revive
sever
voyage

Determining Meanings

Circle the letter next to each answer choice that correctly completes the sentence. There may be more than one correct answer.

1. The **gales**
   (a) were strong enough to blow roofs off.
   (b) blew open when the wind picked up.
   (c) drew a huge crowd on opening night.
   (d) of laughter during the movie were enormous.

2. You **revived**
   (a) a friendship that you miss.
   (b) hope in someone who was ready to give up.
   (c) an object that you lost.
   (d) old memories when you were talking with friends.

3. People study **navigation**
   (a) to learn more about earthquakes.
   (b) so pilots can safely fly airplanes.
   (c) so they can build stronger roads and bridges.
   (d) to become a ship's captain.

4. Things **deteriorated**
   (a) in the oven and smelled delicious.
   (b) when they weren't taken care of.
   (c) in clusters as they grew.
   (d) the more you took care of them.

5. The **destination**
   (a) of the *Mayflower* was Jamestown, but it landed on Cape Cod.
   (b) of falling rain felt good on my skin.
   (c) was caused by a fire in the attic.
   (d) was clearly marked on the front of the bus.

6. The **approximate**
   (a) distance between Earth and the sun is sixty-three million miles.
   (b) age of the Great Pyramid is fifty-five hundred years.
   (c) sound of the thunderstorm scared the dog.
   (d) facts in the article were absolutely true.

7. The **departure**

   (a) was signed by Benjamin Franklin, making it very valuable.

   (b) of the bus was ten minutes late.

   (c) was pulled by two horses.

   (d) in the phone broke when Kal dropped it.

8. The **despairing**

   (a) look in her eyes was easy to see.

   (b) coconuts grow only in tropical countries.

   (c) bus took off right on time.

   (d) howl of the dog when its owner left the house was sad to hear.

4D Completing Sentences

Complete the sentences to demonstrate your knowledge of the words in bold.

| accurate |
| approximate |
| course |
| depart |
| despair |
| destination |
| deteriorate |
| gale |
| horizon |
| jubilation |
| navigate |
| nostalgia |
| revive |
| sever |
| voyage |

1. An example of something that can **deteriorate** is

   _____.

2. If I were caught in a **gale,** I would

   _____.

3. I sometimes feel **nostalgic** for

   _____.

4. I would love to take a **voyage** to

   _____.

5. An **accurate** description of me would be

   _____.

6. I would be **jubilant** if

   _____.

7. If something is **approximate,** that means it is

   _____.

8. If I'm at the park and it starts to rain, my best **course** would be to

   _____.

9. When a kind of clothing from the past is **revived,** that means it is

_____.

10. If I had my own spaceship, my **destination** would be

_____.

4E Vocabulary in Context

Read the passage.

A Difficult Journey

In England in the early seventeenth century, people were not permitted to worship as they pleased; this was a decision made for them by the government. Those who did not like these religious laws were free to emigrate. So, on September 6, 1620, a sailing ship called the *Mayflower* **departed** from Plymouth, England, with 102 passengers.

Many of those on board were leaving to be free to worship in their own way and follow their own religious and spiritual beliefs. Later, they were known as Pilgrims. That is the name for people who make long journeys because of a deep religious faith. Others on the ship were there in the expectation of making a new life for themselves in the new world of America. The passengers, however, did not want to **sever** all connections with England. They had to pay back the money they had borrowed to finance this journey. They intended to do this by engaging in commerce through trade with the old country.

The *Mayflower's* **destination** was Virginia. Early pioneers from England had settled there thirteen years before. But getting there was no straightforward matter. In those days, when sailors were out of sight of land, they **navigated** by measuring the position of the sun and stars. When the sun's position indicated that it was noon, the clocks on board the ship would show a different time, which depended on how far east or west they had traveled. The difference in time was used to calculate their position. But their timepieces and other nautical instruments were not very **accurate.** When clouds obscured the sun or stars, figuring out where they were and in what direction they were headed was not easy.

For the first couple of weeks of the *Mayflower's* **voyage,** gentle breezes carried the ship along; the passengers sat on deck and enjoyed the sunshine. Later on, however, the weather abruptly **deteriorated.** Strong **gales** rocked the *Mayflower* and made life miserable for the passengers; many people became sick. One person developed a fever and died; he was buried at sea. A woman named Elizabeth Hopkins had a baby while the ship was still mid-ocean. She named the child Oceanus. Day after day, the Pilgrims stared forlornly at the **horizon.** They were hoping for a glimpse of land to **revive** their spirits. Day after day, all they saw was the endless sea and the vast sky. Many **despaired** of ever reaching America. Then at last, after sixty-five days, they observed land. That day there was great **jubilation** on board the *Mayflower*.

The Pilgrims soon determined, however, that they had been blown far off their proper **course** by exceptionally strong winds in the mid-Atlantic Ocean. Instead of landing in Virginia, their calculations revealed that they had landed on Cape Cod, **approximately** five hundred miles to the north. For several weeks they explored the coast of Cape Cod Bay, looking for a place to settle. They had precious little time to find a place to build their homes because the bitterly cold winter weather was almost upon them.

Finally, in late December, they discovered a suitable spot. The passengers were conveyed ashore to plan the new settlement and construct houses. The location they selected had been visited earlier by English explorers. The name the explorers had given it may have made some of the Pilgrims **nostalgic;** it was called Plymouth.

accurate
approximate
course
depart
despair
destination
deteriorate
gale
horizon
jubilation
navigate
nostalgia
revive
sever
voyage

▶ **Answer each of the following questions with a sentence. If a question does not contain a vocabulary word from the lesson's word list, use one in your answer. Use each word only once.**

1. What option was open to people in England who wanted to practice their own religion?

_____

_____

2. What is the meaning of **sever** as it is used in the passage?

_____

_____

3. How long did it take the *Mayflower* to get from England to Cape Cod?

_____

_____

4. Where did those on board the *Mayflower* intend to land?

_____

_____

5. What is the meaning of **accurate** as it is used in the passage?

_____

_____

6. **Approximately** how many passengers were there on the *Mayflower?*

_____

_____

7. When did the weather start to get worse?

_____

_____

8. When might it have been dangerous for passengers to go on deck?

_____

_____

9. Why did many passengers **despair** of reaching America?

_____

_____

10. What problem would cloudy skies cause for the crew of the *Mayflower?*

_____

_____

11. Where did the passengers first see land?

_____

_____

12. What is the meaning of **revive** as it is used in the passage?

_____

_____

13. How might the religious Pilgrims have expressed their **jubilation** at seeing land?

_____

_____

14. Name some of the things that the Pilgrims might have felt **nostalgia** for.

_____

_____

15. What **course** was open to the Pilgrims when they found themselves on Cape Cod instead of in Virginia?

_____

_____

| accurate |
| approximate |
| course |
| depart |
| despair |
| destination |
| deteriorate |
| gale |
| horizon |
| jubilation |
| navigate |
| nostalgia |
| revive |
| sever |
| voyage |

Fun & Fascinating FACTS

- Don't confuse **course,** a noun that has several meanings, with the adjective _coarse,_ which means "rough to the touch; crude; not fine." These two words are homophones; they are pronounced the same but have different meanings and spellings.

- Both **revive** and _survive_ (Word List 3) come from the Latin word _vivus,_ which means "living; alive."

- Winds have different names, depending on the speed at which they blow. A _breeze_ goes from 4 miles per hour (a light breeze) to 31 m.p.h. (a strong breeze). A **gale** has a wind speed of from 32 to 63 m.p.h. A _storm_ is a wind blowing between 64 and 73 m.p.h. A _hurricane_ has a wind speed of 74 m.p.h. and higher.

accurate

adjective 1. Measured or calculated correctly.

2. Correct; without mistakes; true in every detail.

. . . .

Academic Context

When doing a science experiment, you must make sure your measurements are **accurate,** or you may end up with an incorrect result.

Word Family

accuracy (noun)
accurately (adverb)

Discussion & Writing Prompt

How can you make sure that your spelling is **accurate?**

2 min.	3 min.
1. Turn and talk to your partner or group.	**2.** Write 2–4 sentences.
Use this space to take notes or draw your ideas.	Be ready to share what you have written.

Review

Hidden Message In the spaces provided to the right of each sentence, write the vocabulary words from Lessons 1 through 4 that are missing in each of the sentences. Be sure that the words you choose fit the meaning of each sentence and have the same number of letters as there are spaces. The number after each sentence is the lesson the word is from. If the exercise is done correctly, the shaded boxes will spell out the answer to this riddle.

How can mail carriers tell how many letters there are in a mailbox without looking inside?

1. I don't let anything _____ me while I'm working. (1)

2. A(n) _____ of mine fought in the Civil War. (3)

3. Cats _____ on mice, chipmunks, and birds. (3)

4. The bus's _____ was New York City. (4)

5. The dog looks _____, but it's quite harmless. (3)

6. Your eyes will soon _____ themselves to the dark. (1)

7. My parents hope to _____ a new car this year. (2)

8. The tires on the bulldozer were _____. (3)

9. We have no other _____ but to continue. (3)

10. The _____ was admitted to the hospital this morning. (1)

11. A(n) _____ dog does not have to be told twice. (1)

12. If I _____ this storm, I'm never going sailing again. (3)

13. Last night's _____ blew several tiles off the roof. (4)

14. My _____ on the trip was my best friend. (1)

15. The speck on the _____ turned out to be an island. (4)

16. I refused to _____ when told to give up my seat. (1)

17. A drink and a short rest will soon _____ us. (4)

18. Give me the _____ day of your arrival. (4)

19. The teacher will _____ you to your new seat. (1)

20. Those trees _____ the view of the lake. (3)

21. Are you and your roommate _____? (1)

22. A large _____ of grapes hung from the vine. (2)

23. The _____ from Seattle to Sydney took a month. (4)

24. A single blow from an ax will _____ the rope. (4)

25. You can _____ mushrooms in any dark, damp place. (2)

26. We will _____ by the stars on our ocean crossing. (4)

27. I felt a sudden wave of _____ for the good old days. (4)

28. A driver needs to be _____ at all times. (1)

29. Do you _____ the meaning of the message? (3)

30. I plan to _____ early as I have to be up at six. (1)

31. Candy canes are very _____, so don't drop any. (2)

32. The _____ we had to follow was laid out for us. (4)

33. I went up and said, "Allow me to _____ myself." (2)

34. You can _____ peaches by canning them. (3)

35. The tiger is a(n) _____ and eats only meat. (3)

36. I'm trying to cut down on the sweets that I _____. (2)

37. The Rockies were a(n) _____ to those heading west. (1)

38. The _____ of popcorn made our mouths water. (2)

39. What is the _____ of a dollar in Mexican money? (2)

40. Wood will _____ if it is not properly cared for. (4)

41. I felt someone in the crowd _____ me. (1)

42. Two _____ men piled the wood in the truck. (1)

43. Sam cannot understand the _____ of how big the universe is. (1)

44. We _____ grain to many countries. (2)

Study the definitions of the words. Then do the exercises that follow.

avalanche
av´ ə lanch

n. 1. A great mass of ice, earth, or snow mixed with rocks sliding down a mountain.
The mountain climbers had a narrow escape when the **avalanche** swept over them.

2. A great amount of something.
The company had an **avalanche** of orders because of their online ad for the new game.

Discuss with your partner how you handle an avalanche of homework.

blizzard
bliz´ ərd

n. A heavy snowstorm with strong winds.
The Chicago airport had to close for two days because of the **blizzard.**

challenge
chal´ ənj

v. 1. To invite others to take part in a contest.
I **challenged** my friend to a game of chess.

2. To cause a person to use a lot of skill or effort.
This trail **challenges** even the best hikers.

3. To question or to argue against, especially when something is unfair or unjust.
Very few scientists **challenge** the idea that a large meteorite killed off the last of the dinosaurs sixty-five million years ago.

n. 1. An interesting task or problem; something that takes skill or effort.
Living out of our backpacks for a week on the mountain was a real **challenge.**

2. A call to take part in a contest.
I accepted the **challenge** to run in the marathon.

Tell your partner which subject challenges you more—reading or math.

conquer
käŋ´ kər

v. 1. To get the better of.
Swimming lessons at the YMCA helped me **conquer** my fear of the water.

2. To defeat.
Our team **conquered** the visiting team, even though our two star players were benched.

conquest *n.* The act of defeating.
The movie was about the **conquest** of Earth by creatures from another planet.

Discuss with your partner how winning a sports event is like a conquest.

crevice
krev´ is

n. A deep, narrow opening in rock caused by a split or crack.
The **crevice** had filled with soil in which a cluster of small red flowers was growing.

foolhardy
fōōl´ här dē

adj. Unwisely bold or daring.
It would be **foolhardy** to go swimming during a gale.

lure
loor

v. To tempt or attract with the promise of something good.
In the early nineteenth century, the hope of owning land of their own **lured** many people to travel west to Ohio and Indiana.

n. 1. Something that attracts.
The **lure** of fresh air led us to the park for a walk.

2. Artificial bait used for fishing.
A large striped bass took the **lure,** and I hooked it.

Talk to your partner about what could lure you to try a new vegetable.

makeshift
māk´ shift

n. A temporary and usually less strong replacement.
We used the camper as a **makeshift** while our house was being built.

adj. Used as a temporary replacement.
We use the cooler as a **makeshift** table when we have a picnic.

optimist
äp´ tə mist

n. One who looks at things in the most positive way; a cheerful, hopeful person.
Jade and Jean are **optimists** and so, of course, they believed the bus would not leave without us.

optimistic *adj.* Cheerful; hopeful.
In spite of the injuries to our best players, I am **optimistic** about our chances of winning the big game.

optimism *n.* A feeling of hope or cheerfulness.
The patients' **optimism** helped them recover more quickly from their illnesses.

Tell your partner if you feel optimistic about the future and why.

previous
prē´ vē əs

adj. Earlier; happening before.
Although I missed the last practice, I attended the two **previous** ones.

Ask your partner if he or she remembers the previous vocabulary word.

route	*n.* 1. The path that must be followed to get to a place.
rōot	Our **route** to Seattle takes us through Denver.
	2. A fixed course or area assigned to a salesperson or delivery person.
	Magali has over a hundred customers on her newspaper **route.**

Talk to your partner about the route you take every day to get to school.

summit	*n.* 1. The highest part; the top.
sum´it	It took us three hours to climb to the **summit** of Mount Washington.
	2. A conference or meeting of the top leaders of governments.
	The **summit** of African heads of state will take place in Nairobi in late June.

terse	*adj.* Short and to the point.
tûrs	When I said I was sure we would be rescued soon, my friend's **terse** reply
	was, "How?"

| thwart | *v.* To block or defeat the plans or efforts of. |
| thwôrt | Heavy flooding **thwarted** the UN's attempts to deliver food. |

| vertical | *adj.* Running straight up and down; upright. |
| vûrt´i kəl | The black **vertical** lines in this painting are what one notices first. |

5A Finding Meanings

Choose two phrases to form a sentence that correctly uses a word from Word List 5. Then write the sentence.

1. (a) the way to reach the top.   (c) A lure is
   (b) a meeting of heads of state.   (d) A summit is

_____

_____

2. (a) An optimistic statement is one   (c) A previous statement is one
   (b) that is released to the public.   (d) that was made earlier.

_____

_____

3. (a) To lure someone is   (c) to offer help or advice to that person.
   (b) To thwart someone is   (d) to tempt that person with promises.

   _____

   _____

4. (a) an area assigned to a   (c) a payment for something done.
       salesperson.
   (b) A crevice is   (d) A route is

   _____

   _____

5. (a) To be thwarted is to be   (c) prevented from carrying out
                                                           one's plans.
   (b) To be challenged is to be   (d) attracted by promises.

   _____

   _____

6. (a) An optimistic report is one (c) that is written out.
   (b) that is hopeful.   (d) A terse report is one

   _____

   _____

7. (a) a call to take part in a contest. (c) A challenge is
   (b) a severe snowstorm with   (d) An avalanche is
       high winds.

   _____

   _____

8. (a) A makeshift file is one that (c) stores things upright.
   (b) A vertical file is one that   (d) gets narrower toward the top.

   _____

   _____

9. (a) A foolhardy remark is one   (c) that sounds threatening.
   (b) that is short and to the point. (d) A terse remark is one

   _____

   _____

avalanche
blizzard
challenge
conquer
crevice
foolhardy
lure
makeshift
optimist
previous
route
summit
terse
thwart
vertical

10. (a) a split or crack in rock.   (c) A blizzard is
    (b) a mass of falling rocks   (d) An avalanche is
        and snow.

_____

_____

Just the Right Word

Replace each phrase in bold with a single word (or form of the word) from the word list.

1. Your **daring but unwise** leap off the boat almost cost you your life.

2. What kind of **artificial bait** is best for catching bluefish?

3. Being appointed chairman was the **highest point** of the general's military career.

4. According to the radio, we can expect a **severe snowstorm with very strong winds** tonight.

5. I'm driving to Yellowstone this summer and wonder which would be the best **way to get there.**

6. The German army's **defeat of the armed forces** of France in 1940 took less than four weeks.

7. A **deep, narrow opening made by a split in the rock** provided a toehold for the climbers making their way up the cliff face.

8. Swimming across the lake will be quite a **difficult task requiring great skill and effort.**

9. What is the reason for Andre's **feeling that all will go well?**

10. Bruno didn't have a pillow, so he used a rolled-up coat as a **temporary replacement for one** and slept quite soundly.

5C

Applying Meanings

Circle the letter or letters next to each correct answer. There may be more than one correct answer.

1. Which of the following might an **optimist** say?
   - (a) "Things could be a lot worse!"
   - (b) "Don't count your chickens."
   - (c) "What's the use?"
   - (d) "I know we can do it."

2. Which of the following might be a **lure** to a person?
   - (a) the Broadway stage
   - (b) the presidency
   - (c) an ocean voyage
   - (d) a tropical island

3. Which of the following might **challenge** a person?
   - (a) competing in the Olympics
   - (b) watching a TV show
   - (c) driving a racing car
   - (d) reading a comic book

4. Of which of the following could there be an **avalanche?**
   - (a) letters
   - (b) orders
   - (c) gales
   - (d) requests

5. Which of the following would you expect to be **vertical?**
   - (a) a sleeping person
   - (b) a front door
   - (c) the horizon
   - (d) a stairway

6. Which of the following might **thwart** someone?
   - (a) support from a friend
   - (b) a sudden change in the weather
   - (c) a flat tire
   - (d) lack of money

7. Which of the following is **foolhardy?**
   - (a) skating on thin ice
   - (b) riding a horse
   - (c) losing your wallet
   - (d) eating salad

8. Which of the following can be **terse?**
   - (a) a comment
   - (b) muscles
   - (c) a phone conversation
   - (d) an aroma

avalanche
blizzard
challenge
conquer
crevice
foolhardy
lure
makeshift
optimist
previous
route
summit
terse
thwart
vertical

Word Study: Suffixes

Complete the questions below.

A prefix comes at the beginning of a word. The part that comes at the end is called a suffix. A suffix can change a word from one part of speech to another. The *-ive* ending changes the verb *create* into the adjective *creative*. The *-or* ending changes it into the noun *creator*. Notice that you may have to add, drop, or change some letters in the word before you add the suffix.

Turn the following verbs into nouns by adding the suffix *-ment*, *-ion*, *-ing*, or *-or*.

1. assign _____

2. distract _____

3. crave _____

4. survive _____

Turn the following nouns into adjectives by adding the suffix *-ic*, *-al*, or *-ous*.

5. optimist _____

6. horizon _____

7. nostalgia _____

8. carnivore _____

Turn the following adjectives into nouns by adding the suffix *-cy*, *-(t)ion*, or *-ence*.

9. accurate _____

10. jubilant _____

11. obedient _____

12. patient _____

On Top of the World

The world's greatest climbers have always been drawn to Mount Everest. In trying to climb it, however, many have been **lured** to their deaths. Everest is located on the border of two Asian countries, Nepal and Tibet. It is part of the Himalayan mountain chain north of India. It is just over twenty-nine thousand feet high. Other mountains are more difficult to climb and offer a greater **challenge.** But because it is the world's highest mountain, Everest has a special place in our imaginations.

Every attempt to reach the top requires careful planning and can cost over a quarter of a million dollars. Often climbers hire Nepalese guides called Sherpas. Sherpas are skilled and experienced mountaineers. Together they work out the **route** to take and set up camps along the way.

Because the air is so thin near the top, climbers need to bring oxygen with them. This adds greatly to the weight that must be carried. In recent years, small groups of climbers have made attempts on Everest without oxygen and without relying on Sherpas. Their daring method has been to travel fast and light. They stay in temporary shelters as they make their way up and down.

Where the mountain rises **vertically,** climbers drive spikes into **crevices** in the rock. Then they pull each other up with ropes. They must be very careful. A loose stone or even a loud noise can start an **avalanche.** An avalanche can bury those caught in its path or sweep them to their deaths. In addition, climbers must be alert to the weather because it can change suddenly for the worse. **Blizzards** often strike with little warning. This forces climbers to scramble for **makeshift** shelter until the danger has passed.

The first people to reach the top of Mount Everest were Edmund Hillary of New Zealand and Tenzing Norgay, his Sherpa guide, in 1953. Teams of mountaineers had made at least eight **previous** tries; but all of them had been **thwarted** in their attempts to stand on the highest spot on Earth. Some had been plagued by bad planning, some by bad weather, and some by bad luck. The first woman to **conquer** Mount Everest was Junko Tabei, of Japan, in 1975; the first American woman to do so was Stacy Allison, in 1988.

avalanche
blizzard
challenge
conquer
crevice
foolhardy
lure
makeshift
optimist
previous
route
summit
terse
thwart
vertical

Mountaineers are by nature **optimists.** They want to believe they will be able to reach the top. At times, however, if either their physical condition or the weather is deteriorating, they are forced to ask themselves if it would be **foolhardy** to continue. Their state of mind plays a big part in this decision. They must sometimes decide when they are only a few hundred feet from the **summit.** Many have chosen to continue, a decision that cost them their lives.

By 2015, Mount Everest had been climbed more than seven thousand times. That year, twenty-two climbers lost their lives making the attempt, the highest ever for a single year. In all, more than 250 people have died trying to reach the top. Why do it if it is so difficult and so dangerous? Someone once put this question to the English climber George Mallory. Mallory had made several unsuccessful tries to climb Mount Everest. He died there with less than six hundred feet to go, in 1924. He had answered the question with the **terse** reply, "Because it's there."

▶ **Answer each of the following questions with a sentence. If a question does not contain a vocabulary word from the lesson's word list, use one in your answer. Use each word only once.**

1. What would you think of someone who planned to climb Mount Everest alone?

_____

_____

2. What is the meaning of **challenge** as it is used in the passage?

_____

_____

3. Why would it be unwise to blow a trumpet while high up on Mount Everest?

_____

_____

4. Why would you expect conversations between climbers to be **terse?**

_____

_____

5. Why do climbers watch the weather carefully?

_____

_____

6. What weather conditions would make a mountain climber **optimistic?**

_____

_____

7. How are **crevices** useful to climbers?

_____

_____

8. What is the meaning of **route** as it is used in the passage?

_____

_____

9. What should people do if caught in bad weather while climbing a mountain?

_____

_____

10. When do climbers need to use ropes?

_____

_____

11. What would happen to a team of climbers who couldn't raise enough money for an attempt on Mount Everest?

_____

_____

12. How did George Mallory explain the **lure** of Mount Everest?

_____

_____

13. Why would Mallory have been familiar with Everest on his last climb?

_____

_____

avalanche
blizzard
challenge
conquer
crevice
foolhardy
lure
makeshift
optimist
previous
route
summit
terse
thwart
vertical

14. How do you suppose climbers know when they have reached the **summit?**

_____

_____

15. Why would climbers feel jubilant while standing on the top of Everest?

_____

_____

Fun & Fascinating FACTS

- Until 1881, a **blizzard** was a loud noise or blast. In that year the *New York Nation* said: "The hard weather has called into use a word which promises to become a national Americanism, namely *blizzard*. It [is the word for] a storm of snow and wind which we cannot resist away from shelter." That is how the word came to have its present meaning. To be called a blizzard, a storm must have winds above thirty-five miles an hour, a temperature close to zero, blowing snow that reduces visibility, and lasts at least three hours.

- The antonym of **optimist** is *pessimist*. Imagine two people looking at a glass of water. The *optimist* thinks the glass is half full; the *pessimist* thinks it is half empty.

- **Route** is sometimes pronounced ROOT and sometimes ROWT; both are correct. Don't confuse this word with *rout,* also pronounced ROWT, which means "a total and complete defeat." *Route* and *root* can be homophones (when both are pronounced ROOT), and so can *route* and *rout* (when both are pronounced ROWT).

- **Vertical** and *horizontal* (Word List 4) are antonyms. In a crossword puzzle, the *horizontal* answers must fit perfectly with the *vertical* answers.

Vocabulary Extension

challenge

verb 1. To invite someone else to take part in a contest against you.

2. To test the ability of a person.

noun An interesting problem; something that tests strength or ability.

Academic Context

In school, your teachers will **challenge** you to learn something new every day.

Word Family

challenger (noun)
challenging (adjective)

Discussion & Writing Prompt

Tell about a time when you **challenged** someone to a competition or when someone else **challenged** you.

2 min.	3 min.
1. Turn and talk to your partner or group.	2. Write 2–4 sentences.
Use this space to take notes or draw your ideas.	Be ready to share what you have written.

Study the definitions of the words. Then do the exercises that follow.

abolish
ə bäl´ ish

v. To bring to an end; to do away with.
Some people support a plan to **abolish** violence in movies.

agony
ag´ ə nē

n. Great pain of mind or body; suffering.
The sprained ankle caused him **agony** for several weeks.

agonizing *adj.* (ag´ ə nīz iŋ) Very painful.
Watching their sick child in the hospital bed was **agonizing** to the parents.

Tell your partner about a time you were in agony when you got hurt.

catapult
kat´ ə pult

n. A machine used in ancient wars that threw objects with great force.
Roman **catapults** could throw six-pound objects almost a third of a mile.

v. To move or be moved suddenly and with great force, as if by a catapult.
The Stones' latest song **catapulted** them to the top of the music charts.

character
kâr´ ək tər

n. 1. The qualities that make a person or place different or special.
Your friend's support during your long illness demonstrates her true **character.**

2. A person in a story, movie, or play.
There are so many **characters** in the book, it's hard to remember who everyone is.

3. A letter or symbol used in writing or printing.
The license-plate number NKT605 contains six **characters.**

Discuss with your partner your favorite character from a TV show or a movie.

denounce
dē nouns´

v. 1. To speak out against something; to criticize.
The principal **denounced** the students who acted out during the school assembly.

2. To accuse someone of doing wrong.
Carla **denounced** Victor, who sat next to her, for cheating on the test.

Talk to your partner about how you would feel if someone denounced you for something you didn't do.

escalate
es´ kə lāt

v. To go up or increase in size or scope.
If house prices continue to **escalate,** many people will be unable to afford to buy a home.

grim
grim

adj. 1. Cruel; fierce.
There were many **grim** battles during the Civil War.

2. Unfriendly or threatening; stern.
The coach's **grim** face expressed his displeasure at our team's poor performance.

3. Unpleasant; disturbing.
We heard the **grim** news that our class hamster has gotten very sick.

Make a grim face at your partner.

harbor
här´bər

n. A protected place along a seacoast where ships can find shelter.
In the summer the **harbor** is busy with sailboats going in and out.

v. 1. To give shelter to; to take care of by hiding.
We **harbored** the injured baby rabbit in my sister's room until our mother found it.

2. To hold and nourish a thought or feeling in the mind.
Try not to **harbor** anger against the person who stole your bike.

inflict
in flikt´

v. To cause something painful to be felt.
The hurricane **inflicted** severe damage on coastal areas.

Tell your partner what you would do if a storm inflicted damage on your home.

loathe
lōth

v. To hate or dislike greatly.
Gandhi, the great Indian leader, **loathed** violence.

loathing *n.* A feeling of hatred.
Their **loathing** of cruelty to animals led them to set up a shelter for unwanted pets.

Discuss with your partner the type of weather you loathe.

meddle
med´əl

v. To involve oneself in other people's affairs without being asked.
When my grandparents retired, they could have **meddled** in my parents' lives, but they didn't.

meddlesome *adj.* Given to taking part in others' affairs without being asked.
If you think I am being **meddlesome,** just tell me to mind my own business.

monstrous	*adj.* 1. Causing shock; horrible; wicked.
män´ strəs	Mikaela begged her parents not to carry out their **monstrous** plan to move her family to another country.
	2. Extremely large.
	A **monstrous** roller coaster was the most exciting ride at the fair.

rouse	*v.* 1. To awaken, to wake up.
rouz	The children were sleeping so soundly that it was difficult to **rouse** them.
	2. To stir up; to excite.
	Martin Luther King Jr. **roused** the American people with his 1963 speech at the Lincoln Memorial in Washington, D.C.

| **steadfast** | *adj.* Unchanging; steady; loyal. |
| sted´ fast | Rigo and Moni remained **steadfast** friends throughout their school years. |

| **translate** | *v.* To put into a different language. |
| trans´ lāt | *The Little Prince*, which was written in French, was **translated** into English by Katherine Woods. |

Tell your partner a word or phrase you can translate from another language.

6A Using Words in Context

Read the following sentences. If the word in bold is used correctly, write C on the line. If the word is used incorrectly, write I on the line.

1. (a) The eggs were **abolished** in the frying pan. _____

(b) Slavery in the United States was **abolished** in 1863. _____

(c) Ancient laws need to be looked at and, in some cases, **abolished.** _____

(d) The old library was torn down, and a new one was **abolished** in its place. _____

2. (a) The novel was written in Spanish but has been **translated** into English. _____

(b) He was **translated** across the street on his skateboard. _____

(c) There's a place online where you can **translate** words. _____

(d) Manuel had **translated** himself into someone we did not recognize. _____

3. (a) The students **harbored** hopes of getting out of school early. _____
   (b) The **harbor** was a safe place for boats to anchor. _____
   (c) We **harbored** the baby bird until it was old enough to fly. _____
   (d) Diego had worked as a **harbor** when he was younger. _____

4. (a) Who is your favorite cartoon **character?** _____
   (b) Help me pry the **character** off this container. _____
   (c) How you treat others shows your true **character.** _____
   (d) I couldn't read the tiny **characters** on the sign at the park. _____

5. (a) The **grim** look on the doctor's face was not a good sign. _____
   (b) Did you hear the **grim** news about my amazing new soccer ball? _____
   (c) Bastian knew from the **grim** way his mother glared at him that he was
       in trouble. _____
   (d) We always bring delicious **grim** food to our annual family reunion. _____

6. (a) The team **roused** all night to rest up for the game the next day. _____
   (b) We were **roused** at four a.m. by the ringing of the alarm bell. _____
   (c) The student **roused** the class with her speech. _____
   (d) The volcano began to **rouse** yesterday morning. _____

7. (a) Shireen is trying to **denounce** her TV time so she can read more. _____
   (b) My teacher **denounces** the idea that homework is a bad thing. _____
   (c) Potato chips were **denounced** by the school parents as unhealthy. _____
   (d) It was **denounced** over the speaker that the bus would depart. _____

8. (a) The statue has been strong and **steadfast** for many years. _____
   (b) When the wind stopped, the boat was **steadfast** in the water. _____
   (c) A dog can be a **steadfast** friend. _____
   (d) This rain has been **steadfast** for five days now. _____

9. (a) Liam was awarded a **meddle** for first place. _____
   (b) The room was such a **meddle,** it took us all day to clean up. _____
   (c) I try never to **meddle** in other people's lives. _____
   (d) **Meddlesome** people do things without asking. _____

10. (a) The **inflict** caused by the tornado wasn't too bad. _____
    (b) The tornado **inflicted** damage on only a few buildings. _____
    (c) I do not want to **inflict** my sickness onto others. _____
    (d) I was **inflicted** with guilt because I didn't help my best friend. _____

abolish

agony

catapult

character

denounce

escalate

grim

harbor

inflict

loathe

meddle

monstrous

rouse

steadfast

translate

6B Making Connections

Circle the letter next to each correct answer. There may be more than one correct answer.

1. Which word or words go with *suffering?*
   (a) character   (b) misery   (c) agony   (d) steadfast

2. Which word or words go with *weapon?*
   (a) beverage   (b) catapult   (c) harbor   (d) horizon

3. Which word or words go with *weather?*
   (a) gale   (b) character   (c) blizzard   (d) hail

4. Which word or words go with *move?*
   (a) elevate   (b) descend   (c) denounce   (d) escalate

5. Which word or words go with *hate?*
   (a) loathe   (b) abolish   (c) detest   (d) revive

6. Which word or words go with *size?*
   (a) meddlesome   (b) gigantic   (c) accurate   (d) monstrous

7. Which word or words go with *cause pain?*
   (a) escalate   (b) impose   (c) inflict   (d) abolish

8. Which word or words go with *sailing?*
   (a) navigate   (b) harbor   (c) voyage   (d) catapult

9. Which word or words go with *strong dislike?*
   (a) detest   (b) meddle   (c) loathe   (d) despise

10. Which word or words go with *imposing?*
    (a) sullen   (b) meddlesome   (c) obstinate   (d) stingy

6C Determining Meanings

Circle the letter next to each answer choice that correctly completes the sentence. There may be more than one correct answer.

1. We **roused** our sisters
   (a) at seven in the morning.
   (b) in separate rooms.
   (c) into cleaning their rooms.
   (d) by telling them we were going to an amusement park.

2. You were **inflicting**
   (a) punishment on someone who had broken the rules.
   (b) harm even though you didn't mean to.
   (c) your best friend in what you were doing.
   (d) the meaning of what I had said.

3. We **loathed**
   (a) the dishes until they were clean.
   (b) the idea of moving somewhere new.
   (c) leaving such a delightful spot, but we had to.
   (d) those scoundrels who tricked people.

4. Each **character**
   (a) in the movie has something to hide.
   (b) on the sign must be easy to see.
   (c) had room for just four people.
   (d) was mixed together to make green paint.

5. The astronauts were **catapulted**
   (a) into space aboard a rocket ship.
   (b) from the rocket into the ocean with a parachute.
   (c) food that didn't taste very good.
   (d) a blanket when it got too cold.

6. His friends were **steadfastly**
   (a) loyal, even though he had let them down.
   (b) staying away from him until he apologized for his rude joke.
   (c) running and stopping because they didn't know where to go.
   (d) changing their minds again and again.

abolish
agony
catapult
character
denounce
escalate
grim
harbor
inflict
loathe
meddle
monstrous
rouse
steadfast
translate

7. A **monstrously**
   (a) large whale surfaced on the water and then dove down again.
   (b) severe storm threatened to wreck dozens of boats.
   (c) false lie was told by Felix about the teacher.
   (d) white piece of paper was on the shelf.

8. Anger **escalated** when
   (a) the elevator got stuck.
   (b) the two best friends wouldn't stop fighting.
   (c) everyone relaxed.
   (d) Tio Domingo accused Felipe of cheating.

6D Completing Sentences

Complete the sentences to demonstrate your knowledge of the words in bold.

1. It would be **agonizing** to

   _____.

2. My favorite fictional **character** is

   _____.

3. Something a **steadfast** friend might do is

   _____.

4. If I could, I would **abolish**

   _____.

5. I would **denounce** a friend if

   _____.

6. A **grim** face looks

   _____.

7. When an argument **escalates,** that means it

   _____.

8. I sometimes **harbor** thoughts about

   _____.

9. A food that I feel **loathing** for is

_____.

10. Right after I **rouse** myself in the morning, I

_____.

Read the passage.

The Pen Is Mightier Than the Sword

In the early nineteenth century, a number of Americans supported slavery, a practice that had been widely accepted since ancient times. Even people who **loathed** slavery, and there were a great many, thought that there was little that one person could do about it. They were wrong. Harriet Beecher Stowe, who was born in Litchfield, Connecticut, in 1811, was someone who caused important changes. She believed that slavery was a **monstrous** crime. While living in Ohio in the 1840s, she used her house to **harbor** enslaved people. These people had escaped from their Southern owners and were making their way north to freedom. In 1850, Harriet moved to Maine with her minister husband. There she wrote a novel called _Uncle Tom's Cabin._ The book not only awakened people to the horrors of slavery but also **catapulted** her to world fame.

Her book painted a **grim** picture of enslaved life. Readers shared the **agony** that the enslaved mother Eliza felt when she accidentally overheard that her only child was to be sold to a slave trader. They eagerly followed Eliza's adventures. First Eliza escaped with her child. Together they crossed the half-frozen Ohio River by jumping from one broken piece of ice to the next. Armed men and yelping dogs were close behind. Readers breathed a sigh of relief when Eliza and her child reached Canada and freedom.

Another **character** in the book is the wise and kindly enslaved man, Uncle Tom. He was sold to Simon Legree. Legree was a man who took pleasure in **inflicting** severe punishment on the people he enslaved. He ordered Uncle Tom to give a whipping to a sick and weak woman who had failed to pick enough cotton. Tom refused. So Legree had him whipped instead. Later, Uncle Tom **steadfastly** refused to tell Legree where two

abolish
agony
catapult
character
denounce
escalate
grim
harbor
inflict
loathe
meddle
monstrous
rouse
steadfast
translate

runaway enslaved people were hiding. Legree had him beaten so severely that he died. Readers wept.

Uncle Tom's Cabin sold millions of copies. It was **translated** into many different languages. It was also made into a stage play. The play was performed all over the world. The book helped **rouse** the people of America, especially those in the North, into demanding an end to slavery. Of course, not everyone looked with favor on *Uncle Tom's Cabin*. It was banned in the South. Slave owners and their supporters accused Harriet Beecher Stowe of **meddling** in their lives. She ignored their protests; she continued to **denounce** slavery in speeches, articles, and books.

The quarrel between the North and the South over the question of slavery **escalated.** In 1863, in the middle of the Civil War, President Abraham Lincoln signed an order **abolishing** slavery in states then under Confederate control. Harriet Beecher Stowe's novel played no small part in bringing about the war that ended slavery. Her life shows that just one determined person can make a difference.

▶ **Answer each of the following questions with a sentence. If a question does not contain a vocabulary word from the lesson's word list, use one in your answer. Use each word only once.**

1. What differing views did Americans have of slavery?

   _____

   _____

2. What happened to the quarrel between the North and the South over slavery?

   _____

   _____

3. What event occurred thirteen years after *Uncle Tom's Cabin* was written?

   _____

   _____

4. Why did Harriet Beecher Stowe suddenly become famous?

   _____

   _____

5. What did Harriet Beecher Stowe believe about slavery?

_____

_____

6. Why were some people who didn't know English able to read *Uncle Tom's Cabin?*

_____

_____

7. Why is it inaccurate to describe Harriet Beecher Stowe as **meddlesome?**

_____

_____

8. How did Harriet Beecher Stowe stand up to the supporters of slavery?

_____

_____

9. What is the meaning of **character** as it is used in the passage?

_____

_____

10. Why do you think Harriet Beecher Stowe wrote *Uncle Tom's Cabin?*

_____

_____

11. What is the meaning of **harbor** as it is used in the passage?

_____

_____

12. How would you say Eliza's **agony** differed from Uncle Tom's?

_____

_____

13. What is it about Simon Legree that makes him so unpleasant?

_____

_____

abolish
agony
catapult
character
denounce
escalate
grim
harbor
inflict
loathe
meddle
monstrous
rouse
steadfast
translate

14. How did Uncle Tom answer when Simon Legree demanded to know where the runaway enslaved people were hiding?

_____

_____

15. What is the meaning of **grim** as it is used in the passage?

_____

_____

Fun & Fascinating FACTS

- Two nouns are formed from the verb **abolish.** *Abolition* is the act of abolishing or the state of being abolished. (It took the terrible Civil War to bring about the *abolition* of slavery in America.) An *abolitionist* is a person who worked to bring about an end to slavery. (William Lloyd Garrison was a famous *abolitionist* who, for thirty-five years, fought to end slavery in America.)

- Don't confuse the verb **loathe** (with a final *-e*) with the adjective *loath* (without the final *-e*) which means "unwilling." (We were having such a good time that we were *loath* to leave.) The *th* sound in *loathe* is pronounced as in *then*; the *th* sound in *loath* is pronounced as in *thin*.

- The homophones **meddle** and *medal* sound alike but have different meanings and spellings. A medal is a small, flat piece of metal given as an honor or to reward bravery.

- The Latin prefix *trans-* means "across" and helps form many English words. A *transatlantic* voyage is one made across the Atlantic Ocean. A radio or television tower *transmits* signals across the land to be picked up by radio and television sets.

- The Latin root *latus* means "to carry" or "to move." It combines with the prefix *trans-* to form **translate.** To translate something is to "move it across" from one language to another.

character

noun 1. A person in a story, movie, or play.

2. The special qualities about a person or a place.

3. A letter, number, or symbol used in writing or printing.

Academic Context

All fictional stories have a setting, a plot, and at least one **character.**

Word Family

characteristic
characteristically
un**character**istic
un**character**istically

Discussion & Writing Prompt

Who is your favorite **character** in the book, and why is this character your favorite?

2 min.	3 min.
1. Turn and talk to your partner or group.	2. Write 2–4 sentences.
Use this space to take notes or draw your ideas.	Be ready to share what you have written.

Word List

Study the definitions of the words. Then do the exercises that follow.

colony
käl´ ə nē

n. 1. A group of people, animals, or plants living close together.
We found a **colony** of ants in the yard.

2. A group of people who settle in a new land and have legal ties to the country they came from.
English people formed a **colony** at Jamestown, Virginia, in 1607.

compensate
käm´ pən sāt

v. 1. To make up for, to be equivalent to.
My parents gave me another bike to **compensate** for the one that was stolen.

2. To pay for.
Our student council voted to **compensate** the students who help clean up the lunchroom.

compensation *n.* Payment to make up for something.
Isa received ten thousand dollars as **compensation** for injuries she suffered when her bike fell apart.

Discuss with your partner how someone might compensate you for returning a lost cell phone.

deposit
dē päz´ it

v. 1. To lay down.
The hikers **deposited** their backpacks on the porch.

2. To put money into a bank account or to give as partial payment.
Sign your name on the back before you **deposit** the check.

n. 1. Something laid down.
The flood left a **deposit** of stones on the riverbanks.

2. Money put into a bank account or given as partial payment.
For a $20 **deposit,** the store will hold the winter coat.

Chat with your partner about how a deposit of snow overnight might mean school is cancelled.

fascinate
fas´ ə nāt

v. To attract; to strongly hold the interest of.
The circus clowns **fascinated** the children in the audience.

fascinating *adj.* Extremely interesting.
The museum has a **fascinating** display of Native American crafts.

feeble
fē´ bəl

adj. 1. Having little strength, weak.
Lions prey on the most **feeble** zebras in the herd.

2. Not very believable or satisfying.
Henry gave the teacher a **feeble** explanation for being late to class: His watch was broken.

. . . .

Tell your partner about a feeble excuse you tried to use to get out of doing chores.

formal
fôr´ məl

adj. 1. Following rules or customs, often in an exact and proper way.
The president gave a **formal** dinner at the White House.

2. Suitable for events where strict standards of dress and behavior are expected.
Ming wanted a **formal** dress for the fancy party.

frigid
frij´ id

adj. 1. Very cold.
The morning air was so **frigid** that her mom's car would not start.

2. Lacking a warm manner; unfriendly.
The **frigid** greeting we received made it clear that we were not welcome.

harsh
härsh

adj. 1. Rough and unpleasant to the senses.
In a **harsh** tone of voice, the farmer ordered us to stay away from the cows.

2. Causing pain; cruel.
My brother's **harsh** words hurt me deeply, and he later told me he was sorry.

3. Not suitable for living things; extremely uncomfortable.
Northern Canada's **harsh** climate keeps people from settling there.

huddle
hud´ əl

v. 1. To crowd together.
When the downpour began, we all **huddled** under one umbrella.

2. To curl one's limbs up close to one's body.
During their first night at camp, Alya and Inez **huddled** under their thin blankets to keep warm.

n. A closely packed group.
The players went into a **huddle** to plan the next play.

remote
rē mōt´

adj. 1. Far away in time or space.
The trail took them through a **remote** region of the Amazon rainforest.

2. Slight or faint.
There was only a **remote** chance of reaching our destination on time.

3. Controlled indirectly or from a distance.
Dad told us to do a better job of sharing the television **remote** control.

4. Distant in manner.
The store clerk seemed very **remote** and hardly looked at us when we asked for help.

Share with your partner an idea you have for a fantastic field trip that has only a remote chance of happening.

---

resemble
rē zem´ bəl

v. To be like or similar to.
The markings on the wings of the moth **resemble** the eyes of a small animal and help protect it from becoming prey.

---

rigid
rij´ id

adj. 1. Stiff and unbending; not flexible.
The frozen rope was as **rigid** as a stick.

2. Strict; not easily changed.
The school has a **rigid** rule that students must wear uniforms.

Talk to your partner about a rigid rule you want to change at school.

---

solitary
säl´ ə ter ē

adj. 1. Being alone; lacking the company of others.
In the nineteenth century, lighthouse keepers often led **solitary** lives.

2. Being the only one.
A **solitary** elm grew in the middle of the field.

Tell your partner how you fill the time when you have a solitary afternoon.

---

substantial
səb stan´ shəl

adj. 1. Strong; solid.
The chair is not **substantial** enough to support the weight of an adult.

2. Great in value or size.
I received a **substantial** increase in my allowance because I agreed to do more chores.

Discuss with your partner a food you can eat a substantial amount of.

waddle	v. To walk with short steps, swaying from side to side.
wäd´əl	The duck left the pond and **waddled** toward us.
	n. An awkward, clumsy walk.
	The baby smiled excitedly as he ended his **waddle** across the room.

7A Finding Meanings

Choose two phrases to form a sentence that correctly uses a word from Word List 7. Then write the sentence.

1. (a) that is operated from a distance.
   (b) that is easy to operate.
   (c) A rigid control is one
   (d) A remote control is one

   _____

   _____

2. (a) To waddle is to
   (b) To huddle is to
   (c) hold a person's interest or attention.
   (d) curl one's limbs up close to one's body.

   _____

   _____

| colony |
| compensate |
| deposit |
| fascinate |
| feeble |
| formal |
| frigid |
| harsh |
| huddle |
| remote |
| resemble |
| rigid |
| solitary |
| substantial |
| waddle |

3. (a) A deposit is
   (b) A colony is
   (c) a group who settles in a new place.
   (d) a payment for a concert ticket.

   _____

   _____

4. (a) To resemble someone
   (b) is to pay that person.
   (c) To compensate someone
   (d) is to apologize to that person.

   _____

   _____

5. (a) one that goes on too long.
   (b) A formal apology is
   (c) one that is difficult to believe.
   (d) A feeble apology is

   _____

   _____

6. (a) is not changed easily.
   (b) A rigid attitude is one that
   (c) A frigid attitude is one that
   (d) is no longer practiced.

   _____

   _____

7. (a) is unpleasantly rough.
   (b) A harsh reply is one that
   (c) is too late to be useful.
   (d) A formal reply is one that

   _____

   _____

8. (a) A fascinating place is one
   (b) that is in the tropics.
   (c) A frigid place is one
   (d) that is very interesting.

   _____

   _____

9. (a) that is open to the public.
   (b) A solitary building is one
   (c) A substantial building is one
   (d) that has no others close to it.

   _____

   _____

10. (a) money given as a payment.
    (b) A deposit is
    (c) a path that one follows.
    (d) A waddle is

    _____

    _____

Just the Right Word

Replace each phrase in bold with a single word (or form of the word) from the word list.

1. From a distance crocodiles **look almost the same as** alligators.

2. Sarita's wind-up toy **swayed from side to side as it took short steps** across the floor.

3. A life that is **lived apart from other people** need not be lonely as long as one has books to read.

4. A **very cold** mass of air from Canada caused this wintry weather.

5. The cast on your broken arm will keep it **in a fixed position and prevent it from bending.**

6. The most **strongly built** of the three houses was the one made of bricks.

7. These patients recovering from operations are so **lacking in strength** that they cannot walk.

8. Meetings with the emperor are very **carefully arranged so as to follow strict rules.**

9. In the **very distant** past all the continents were joined together.

10. After playing in the snow all day, we **crowded close together** around the fire to get warm.

colony
compensate
deposit
fascinate
feeble
formal
frigid
harsh
huddle
remote
resemble
rigid
solitary
substantial
waddle

7C

Applying Meanings

Circle the letter or letters next to each correct answer. There may be more than one correct answer.

1. Which of the following can be **compensated?**
   - (a) an injured person
   - (b) a worker
   - (c) a person suffering a loss
   - (d) a victim of a crime

2. Which of the following might be **formal?**
   - (a) a joke
   - (b) a dance
   - (c) a request
   - (d) a bow

3. Which of the following might be **substantial?**
   - (a) a meal
   - (b) the horizon
   - (c) a sum of money
   - (d) a purchase

4. Which of the following can be found in **colonies?**
   - (a) settlers
   - (b) islands
   - (c) ants
   - (d) mountains

5. Which of the following can be **deposited?**
   - (a) money in a bank
   - (b) eggs in a nest
   - (c) answers on a test
   - (d) books on a table

6. Which of the following **resembles** a horse?
   - (a) a zebra
   - (b) a giraffe
   - (c) a mule
   - (d) a donkey

7. Which of the following moves with a **waddle?**
   - (a) a snake
   - (b) a frog
   - (c) a duck
   - (d) an ostrich

8. Which of the following can be **harsh?**
   - (a) a climate
   - (b) a punishment
   - (c) a voice
   - (d) a reward

Word Study: Antonyms

Write the antonym of each of the words on the left in the space next to it. Choose from the words on the right, which are in a different order.

1. harsh _____ joy

2. agony _____ tropical

3. feeble _____ love

4. escalate _____ disloyal

5. deposit _____ flexible

6. rigid _____ withdraw

7. fascinating _____ fall

8. frigid _____ burly

9. steadfast _____ gentle

10. loathe _____ boring

colony
compensate
deposit
fascinate
feeble
formal
frigid
harsh
huddle
remote
resemble
rigid
solitary
substantial
waddle

Birds in Tuxedos

What is a bird? A creature that flies, of course. And yet, penguins are birds, but they cannot fly. Their wings are too **feeble** to lift them off the ground. This was not always so. Scientists believe that penguins once flew just like other birds. At some time in the **remote** past, they migrated to Antarctica. That is the frozen land that surrounds the South Pole. The ice sheet there is two miles thick in places. The temperature varies between zero in summer and negative seventy degrees in winter. It is possible that penguins were the only creatures that could survive in such a **harsh** climate. Without enemies, they would have no need to use their wings, as other birds do, to escape attacks. Gradually, they would have lost the ability to fly.

Over many thousands of years, the wings of penguins became smaller and more **rigid.** To **compensate** for the loss, it seems, they became excellent swimmers. They use their wings as flippers. Their webbed feet help guide them through the water. They can dive to depths of seventy feet and often leap high out of the water for a breath of air. On land, they **waddle** awkwardly or slide along the ice on their stomachs. But under water they glide gracefully and effortlessly. Penguins spend a lot of time in the sea in a never-ending search for fish, lobster, crabs, and shrimp. These foods make up a **substantial** part of their diet.

There are several different kinds of penguins. The smallest is no bigger than a duck. The largest, called the Emperor penguin, is four feet tall and weighs up to ninety pounds. In addition to the shores of Antarctica, penguins make their homes farther north. They live on the coasts of South Africa, Australia, and New Zealand, or on the Pacific coast of South America.

Each year for several months, penguins come to land to make nests and lay their eggs. Along the shores of Antarctica, where no plants grow, the penguins gather stones for their nests. Females **deposit** the eggs, chalky white in color and usually no more than two, on the nest. Emperor penguins do not build nests. Instead, after an egg is laid, the male penguin holds it on his feet under a fold of stomach skin. This keeps the egg warm. The female Emperor penguin returns to the **frigid** waters to hunt for food for her family.

For two months, the baby penguins develop in the eggs. All that time the male Emperor penguins **huddle** close together in **colonies** of up to half a million birds so that they can keep warm. A **solitary** penguin would soon lose its body heat and die in the freezing cold of the long Antarctic night. When the baby penguins break out of the shells, they are unable to see and are quite helpless. For several months they have to be fed by their parents before they are ready to take to the water to find their own food.

On land penguins are unlikely to be mistaken for any other kind of bird. With black feathers covering their backs and snowy white feathers running up their fronts, they **resemble** very short men wearing **formal** dress. Their appearance, combined with the way they walk, makes them look slightly comical. Perhaps this explains in part why we humans find them such **fascinating** creatures.

▶ **Answer each of the following questions with a sentence. If a question does not contain a vocabulary word from the lesson's word list, use one in your answer. Use each word only once.**

1. Why are penguins a popular feature in aquariums and zoos?

_____

_____

2. What is the meaning of **deposit** as it is used in the passage?

_____

_____

3. In what way do penguins not **resemble** other kinds of birds?

_____

_____

4. What strikes some people as comical about a penguin's appearance?

_____

_____

5. Why did penguins' wings become so **feeble?**

_____

_____

colony
compensate
deposit
fascinate
feeble
formal
frigid
harsh
huddle
remote
resemble
rigid
solitary
substantial
waddle

6. How would you describe the summer temperatures of Antarctica?

_____

_____

7. In what way does the passage suggest that penguins were **compensated** for losing the ability to fly?

_____

_____

8. Where do penguins spend much of their time?

_____

_____

9. According to the passage, were penguins ever able to fly?

_____

_____

10. What is the meaning of **rigid** as it is used in the passage?

_____

_____

11. Which details in the passage illustrate the **harsh** climate of Antarctica?

_____

_____

12. Why do Emperor penguins gather in large **colonies?**

_____

_____

13. Describe the contrast between the way penguins move on land and in water.

_____

_____

14. What is the meaning of **huddle** as it is used in the passage?

_____

_____

15. What would happen to a penguin that wandered off by itself while on land?

_____

_____

Fun & Fascinating FACTS

- The adjective formed from **colony** is *colonial*. (Virginia was one of the thirteen American *colonies* that declared their independence from British rule in 1776. The town of Williamsburg, Virginia, re-creates life in *colonial* America.)

  Note that *colony* can also refer to a group of people, especially artists and writers, who come together in a particular place. There they can meet and exchange ideas while working without distractions.

- **Remote** and *distant* are synonyms. Both words mean "far off in distance or time." *Remote,* however, also suggests something cut off and out of the way. Tristan da Cunha, an island in the South Atlantic, and Tokyo, Japan, are each *distant* from New York. But Tokyo is not considered a *remote* city, because it is easy to get to by plane. Tristan da Cunha, however, is thought of as a *remote* island because it is difficult to get to.

- **Solitary** is formed from the Latin *solus,* which means "alone." Several other words are formed from the same Latin root. *Solitude* is "the quality or state of being alone." (Henry David Thoreau was seeking *solitude* when he lived alone in the woods near Walden Pond.) *Isolated* means "cut off from the company of others." (We felt *isolated* when the blizzard kept us inside for three days.) *Solitaire* is a card game for just one person.

colony

compensate

deposit

fascinate

feeble

formal

frigid

harsh

huddle

remote

resemble

rigid

solitary

substantial

waddle

rigid

adjective 1. Not flexible.

2. Strict; not easily changed.

. . . .

Context Clues

These sentences give clues to the meaning of **rigid.**

*We put the soft sandwiches in a hard-sided cooler. Its **rigid** sides would protect our lunch from getting squished.*

*We have a **rigid** schedule each morning before school, but after school our schedule is more relaxed.*

Synonyms and Antonyms

Synonyms: inflexible, solid, stiff, strict
Antonyms: flexible, soft, floppy, loose

Discussion & Writing Prompt

Give an example of something on your desk or table that is **rigid** and something that is flexible.

2 min.	3 min.
1. Turn and talk to your partner or group.	2. Write 2–4 sentences.
Use this space to take notes or draw your ideas.	Be ready to share what you have written.

Word List

Study the definitions of the words. Then do the exercises that follow.

assemble
ə sem´ bəl

v. 1. To bring together into a group; to gather.
At two o'clock we **assembled** at the door of the museum for a tour.

2. To put or fit together.
You need only a screwdriver to **assemble** the bookcase.

assembly *n.* 1. A group of people gathered for a certain purpose.
At the **assembly** this morning, the fire chief will talk to us about fire prevention.

2. The fitting together of various parts.
The **assembly** of the new desk took less than an hour.

Tell your partner about something you have seen assembled or helped to assemble, such as a bicycle.

banquet
baŋ´ kwət

n. A large meal for many people; a feast.
Fancy foods were served at the **banquet,** which was given in honor of the teachers who were retiring.

cargo
kär´ go

n. The load carried by a plane or ship.
The **cargo** going to Chile was put into containers and loaded onto the boat.

cask
kask

n. A barrel-shaped container, especially one for holding liquids.
In the 1800s, ships carried drinking water for the sailors in large **casks.**

celebrate
sel´ ə brāt

v. To honor something in a special way.
Americans **celebrate** the signing of the Declaration of Independence every Fourth of July.

celebrated *adj.* Famous.
Marian Anderson, the **celebrated** African American singer, performed on the steps of the Lincoln Memorial in Washington, D.C.

Share with your partner a celebrated person you would like to meet.

decrease
di krēs´

v. To become smaller or less.
After June 22, the length of the day gradually **decreases.**

n. (dē´ krēs) The amount by which something becomes smaller.
An outbreak of flu caused a **decrease** in school attendance during January.

Tell your partner if you want to increase or decrease the amount of television you watch, and why.

desperate
des´ pər ət

adj. 1. Reckless because of feelings of despair.
The action star in the movie jumped from a five-story building in a **desperate** attempt to escape her captors.

2. So serious as to be almost hopeless.
The situation of the homeless in our big cities is becoming increasingly **desperate.**

Discuss with your partner how a desperate animal might act if it was trapped.

edible
ed´ ə bəl

adj. Safe or fit to be eaten.
Are you certain those mushrooms are **edible?**

n. An item of food; anything that can be eaten.
We'll serve the beverages at this end of the table and the sandwiches and other **edibles** at the other end.

frivolous
friv´ ə ləs

adj. Not serious or important; silly.
Spending money on items like comic books seems **frivolous.**

frivolity *n.* (fri väl´ ə tē) Silly or lighthearted play.
The giggling children had to be reminded that there is no place for **frivolity** during detention.

Talk to your partner about a frivolous way to spend your time on weekends.

harvest
här´ vəst

n. 1. The gathering of ripe crops for a season.
In Spain, the grape **harvest** begins in late summer.

2. The quantity of crops gathered.
Iowa's corn **harvest** is the largest in years.

v. To gather in the crops.
We usually **harvest** the first peas in April.

hew
hyōō

v. 1. To chop down or cut with blows from an ax.
Let's **hew** these dead branches from the tree before they fall and cause damage.

2. To cut or shape with blows of an ax or similar tool.
The Tlingit of the Northwest **hewed** totem poles from tree trunks.

| **hostile** | *adj.* Unfriendly; of or like an enemy. |
| häs´ təl | The **hostile** audience would not permit the speaker to finish the speech. |

hostility *n.* The expression of unfriendly feelings.
The governor's plan to close the neighborhood school met with so much **hostility** that it was quickly dropped.

....

Chat with your partner about the best way to react to someone who treats you with hostility.

| **pledge** | *v.* To make a serious promise. |
| plej | A dozen local store owners have **pledged** their support for the new arts program. |

n. A serious promise.
Our class signed a **pledge** to respect one another.

| **prosper** | *v.* To succeed, especially in terms of money. |
| präs´ pər | Alaska **prospered** when oil was found there. |

prosperous *adj.* Enjoying growth and success.
The **prosperous** family always helps people who are having a tough time.

| **task** | *n.* A piece of work that needs to be done. |
| task | Cutting our way through the jungle was a difficult **task.** |

....

Talk to your partner about your least favorite task, such as doing the dishes or making your bed.

8A

Using Words in Context

Read the following sentences. If the word in bold is used correctly, write C on the line. If the word is used incorrectly, write I on the line.

1. (a) Each camper was given a **task** to perform. _____
   (b) When I had the flu, getting out of bed was a difficult **task.** _____
   (c) **Tasks** were easy for Theo, who was good at everything he tried. _____
   (d) I tried to brush the **task** every day. _____

2. (a) The students will **assemble** in the hallway. _____
   (b) I was able to **assemble** the puzzle in less than ten minutes. _____
   (c) They tell me that I **assemble** my cousin because we both are blonde. _____
   (d) The **assembly** of new cars is done by machines. _____

3. (a) We **celebrate** the Fourth of July with fireworks. _____
   (b) I was feeling **celebrated,** so I lay down for a while. _____
   (c) We **celebrated** my new baby brother with a party. _____
   (d) Abraham Lincoln is a **celebrated** name in U.S. history. _____

4. (a) Apples are usually **harvested** in October. _____
   (b) This year's **harvest** should be the biggest in years. _____
   (c) We found out that **harvests** like colored pencils and chalk. _____
   (d) I **harvested** the bed before I slept in it. _____

5. (a) The **cargo** is dragged into the truck every morning. _____
   (b) Each student is allowed to eat one **cargo.** _____
   (c) The **cargo** plane took off with a heavy load. _____
   (d) I need to be in the **cargo** by 7:30 a.m., or I will be late for school. _____

6. (a) The **decrease** in the number of monarch butterflies is sad. _____
   (b) If we **decrease** the price of apples, we expect to sell more. _____
   (c) The teacher **decreased** that the test was cancelled. _____
   (d) We need to **decrease** the number of balloons at the party. _____

7. (a) The **desperate** way I feel is very joyful. _____
   (b) The kitten that ran up the tree was **desperate** to be rescued. _____
   (c) After the earthquake, there was a **desperate** need for medical
       supplies. _____
   (d) Wes played a **desperate** amount of time at the park. _____

8. (a) The actress didn't like to be asked **frivolous** questions. _____
   (b) The magazine was full of **frivolous** stories about movie stars. _____
   (c) Taking care of someone who is sick is very **frivolous.** _____
   (d) Certain vegetables are extremely **frivolous** and should not be
       eaten. _____

9. (a) Yesterday's pizza is still **edible,** so go ahead and eat it. _____

(b) These stories are **edible** for children under five years old. _____

(c) Her story was too **inedible** to be true. _____

(d) Horses like fresh grass, but they think hay is **edible** also. _____

10. (a) My little sister sometimes has a **hostile** attitude that is very unfriendly. _____

(b) There was much **hostility** from the community when the government decided to close the park. _____

(c) A **hostile** in the middle of the sidewalk blocked our bikes. _____

(d) The **hostile** of the party made sure we had lots of food and drink. _____

8B Making Connections

Circle the letter next to each correct answer. There may be more than one correct answer.

1. Which word or words go with *meals?*

(a) banquet   (b) edible   (c) cargo   (d) beverage

2. Which word or words go with *container?*

(a) pledge   (b) vessel   (c) cask   (d) harvest

3. Which word or words go with *weak?*

(a) edible   (b) feeble   (c) hostile   (d) puny

4. Which word or words go with *cut?*

(a) hew   (b) sever   (c) gash   (d) task

5. Which word or words go with *promise?*

(a) celebrate   (b) assemble   (c) abolish   (d) pledge

6. Which word or words go with *do well?*

(a) prosper   (b) decrease   (c) thrive   (d) denounce

assemble
banquet
cargo
cask
celebrate
decrease
desperate
edible
frivolous
harvest
hew
hostile
pledge
prosper
task

7. Which word or words go with *full of hate?*

  (a) malicious (b) edible (c) frivolous (d) hostile

8. Which word or words go with *farm?*

  (a) harvest (b) meadow (c) orchard (d) cargo

9. Which word or words go with *less?*

  (a) decrease (b) escalate (c) reduce (d) celebrate

10. Which word or words go with *not serious?*

  (a) fierce (b) desperate (c) prosperous (d) frivolous

8C Determining Meanings

Circle the letter next to each answer choice that correctly completes the sentence. There may be more than one correct answer.

1. The students are **assembling**
   (a) in the lunchroom.
   (b) the new table from the parts in the box.
   (c) what happened when the bus ran out of gas.
   (d) each other when they wear similar shirts.

2. The **casks**
   (a) are very heavy when they are full.
   (b) are worn on the head to protect the skull.
   (c) neared the finish line.
   (d) hold forty gallons of juice.

3. I **desperately**
   (a) cried for help when I almost dropped the heavy box.
   (b) swung the bat and ended up with a home run.
   (c) attempted to reach the pool before it closed.
   (d) yawned and lay down in bed slowly.

4. Let's **hew**
    (a) the logs with axes so we can have a fire in the fireplace later.
    (b) two pieces of paper together with glue.
    (c) the books to get ready for the quiz.
    (d) our way to school every day.

5. Trevon **pledged**
    (a) up the hill.
    (b) that he would always be kind to his little sister.
    (c) the pencil to keep it sharp.
    (d) the note so he wouldn't forget it.

6. I was **tasked**
    (a) with stretching after a nap.
    (b) with taking care of the class rabbit.
    (c) with hearing that they were laughing at what I had said.
    (d) with researching about animals that hibernate in the winter.

7. They **frivolously**
    (a) skipped around the track singing songs.
    (b) wrote a report about British authors.
    (c) smiled and passed notes across the table.
    (d) made sure the dog had enough food.

8. Our **celebration**
    (a) was for the firefighters who saved the school.
    (b) ended up lasting late into the night.
    (c) device kept us floating on the water.
    (d) machine was old and rusty.

assemble
banquet
cargo
cask
celebrate
decrease
desperate
edible
frivolous
harvest
hew
hostile
pledge
prosper
task

8D Completing Sentences

Complete the sentences to demonstrate your knowledge of the words in bold.

1. Something I have **prospered** at is

   _____.

2. Something you might find at a **banquet** is

   _____.

3. A **celebrated** person I would like to meet is

   _____.

4. My favorite **edible** is

   _____.

5. An example of a **frivolous** remark might be

   _____.

6. An example of a **hostile** remark might be

   _____.

7. I **pledge** to

   _____.

8. My most important **task** at home is

   _____.

9. If you are **desperate** to eat something, that means you are

   _____.

10. The opposite of **decrease** is

    _____.

Vocabulary in Context
Read the passage.

The First Thanksgiving

The hundred or so Pilgrims and other passengers who left England in 1620 aboard the *Mayflower* arrived at Plymouth, in what is now Massachusetts. Before going ashore, the forty-one male passengers **assembled** in the ship's main cabin. There they wrote the Mayflower Compact. Under this agreement, everyone, Pilgrims and non-Pilgrims alike, would be governed by the same laws. All those present **pledged** to observe the Compact.

The Pilgrims had come ashore at the end of December. They had to work fast to prepare for winter. Their first **task** was to build shelter to keep themselves safe from animals and bad weather. Soon the sound of axes rang out as trees were chopped down and **hewed** into logs. Next, the *Mayflower's* **cargo** had to be unloaded. There were root vegetables and lemons in crates, sacks of sugar and flour, and cider in **casks.** Also onboard were slabs of salt pork and beef, and seeds for planting in the spring. There were small items of furniture, and chests packed with blankets, linens, and clothes. There were family Bibles and tools of all kinds. But there were no musical instruments—the Pilgrims considered music and dancing to be **frivolous**.

That first winter was a grim one. Food was scarce. Many people became sick and died. By the time the *Mayflower* sailed back to England in the early spring, the number of people remaining had **decreased** to fewer than sixty. Many of that group were too feeble to work. Those who had survived the winter were also worried that the Native Americans would be **hostile** toward them as new settlers.

One spring day they were very surprised when a Native American walked into their settlement and greeted them in English. His name was Samoset; he explained that he had learned English from sea captains who had earlier explored the Atlantic coast. He told them of another man, Squanto, who also spoke English. A week or so later he returned with Squanto and sixty Wampanoags, who lived nearby. The colonists were glad that their visitors were friendly. With their food almost gone, their situation was **desperate.**

assemble
banquet
cargo
cask
celebrate
decrease
desperate
edible
frivolous
harvest
hew
hostile
pledge
prosper
task

Because of the help of these native people, the colonists quickly learned which berries and other fruits were **edible.** They learned where to catch fish, and the best way to grow corn, beans, and squash. When they needed to talk with other native people, Squanto often acted as their translator.

Later in 1621, after the first **harvest,** the colonists held a **banquet** and invited Massasoit, the leader of the Wampanoags, to bring his people to **celebrate** with them. This was the first Thanksgiving; it lasted three days. The worst was now over for the colonists. When the *Mayflower* returned in 1622, it brought more people to join the colony. It also carried precious supplies. More ships arrived in the following years; the Plymouth colony grew in size and began to **prosper.** Its future was no longer in doubt.

▶ **Answer each of the following questions with a sentence. If a question does not contain a vocabulary word from the lesson's word list, use one in your answer. Use each word only once.**

1. What do Americans today do to remember the large dinner that took place at Plymouth in 1621?

_____

_____

2. If the Pilgrims were alive today, what do you suppose they might think of rock concerts?

_____

_____

3. What did the *Mayflower* carry besides the passengers and crew?

_____

_____

4. What **task** did the forty-one male passengers complete before going ashore?

_____

_____

5. What is the meaning of **assembled** as it is used in the passage?

_____

_____

6. What valuable information did the Native Americans give the colonists?

_____

_____

7. What is the meaning of **hewed** as it is used in the passage?

_____

_____

8. Why was it likely that the colonists would obey the rules set out in the Mayflower Compact?

_____

_____

9. What beverage might have been served at the **banquet?**

_____

_____

10. What would happen to the contents of a **cask** if it got a hole in it?

_____

_____

11. What might the colonists have **harvested** in 1621?

_____

_____

12. In what way did the Native Americans surprise the colonists?

_____

_____

13. How many colonists survived the first winter?

_____

_____

14. Why might the survivors of the first winter have felt **desperate?**

_____

_____

15. How do you think life in the colony changed as it **prospered?**

_____

_____

| assemble |
| banquet |
| cargo |
| cask |
| celebrate |
| decrease |
| desperate |
| edible |
| frivolous |
| harvest |
| hew |
| hostile |
| pledge |
| prosper |
| task |

Fun & Fascinating FACTS

- The antonym of **edible** is *inedible*. (The food was so overcooked that it was *inedible*.) Another antonym is *poisonous*. (Cultivated mushrooms are *edible*, but some wild mushrooms are *poisonous*.)

- Don't confuse **hew** with *hue*, which is a color or shade of color. (Aqua is a blue color with a greenish *hue*.) These two words are homophones; they are pronounced the same but have different meanings and spellings.

- **Pledge** and *promise* are synonyms, but a pledge is a serious promise, made concerning something important. You might *promise* to meet a friend after school; you *pledge* allegiance to the flag of the United States.

task

noun A piece of work that must be done.

To-Do List
☑ make bed
☑ feed cat
☐ trash out
☐ homework

Academic Context

In school, you will do many **tasks** each day, such as solving math problems, writing sentences, or taking care of the class pet.

Synonyms

chore, duty, job

Discussion & Writing Prompt

Describe a few of the **tasks** you have to do at home.

2 min.	3 min.
1. Turn and talk to your partner or group.	2. Write 2–4 sentences.
Use this space to take notes or draw your ideas.	Be ready to share what you have written.

Review

Crossword Puzzle   Solve the crossword puzzle by studying the clues and filling in the answer boxes. The number after a clue is the lesson the word is from.

Clues Across

1. The highest part (5)
6. To become less or fewer (8)
7. Opposite of *strong*
9. Lacking strength (7)
10. The largest city in Nebraska
14. To put into a different language (6)
15. Short for "New York City"
18. A cheerful, hopeful person (5)
21. To hate or despise (6)
22. The way to get to a place (5)
23. To promise (8)
24. Safe to eat (8)
25. To gather in crops (8)

Clues Down

2. Used as a temporary replacement (5)
3. To cause to bear something painful (6)
4. Unpleasant; disturbing (6)
5. To chop or cut down with an ax (8)
8. Great pain and suffering (6)
11. Unfriendly (8)
12. Very wicked; terrible (6)
13. To succeed; to do well (8)
16. A deep narrow opening (5)
17. To walk with an awkward, swaying movement (7)
19. A large country in Asia
20. To tempt with a promise of something (5)

Study the definitions of the words. Then do the exercises that follow.

absurd
ab surd´

adj. So unreasonable as to be laughable; foolish or silly.
You'd look **absurd** in a suit and tie at the beach.

Tell your partner an absurd idea, like an elephant riding a motorcycle or a cat becoming president.

accomplish
ə käm´ plish

v. To do something by making an effort; to complete successfully.
I know I will **accomplish** these errands by noon.

accomplishment *n.* Something requiring skill and determination that is completed successfully.
Anne Sullivan's great **accomplishment** was to teach a child who was deaf and blind to speak and to read.

Share with your partner something you want to accomplish this year.

ascend
ə send´

v. To rise, usually in a steady way.
The rocket **ascended** to a height of five hundred feet before falling to Earth.

dense
dens

adj. 1. Tightly packed; crowded close together.
The tired explorers hacked their way through **dense** vines and bushes to reach the coast.

2. Thick; hard to see through.
At the airport there was such **dense** fog that planes couldn't take off.

3. Stupid, thickheaded.
I don't want to seem **dense,** but I don't understand your question.

Tell your partner how you feel when you are walking in a dense crowd of people.

experiment
ek sper´ ə mənt

n. A test to prove or discover something.
The **experiment** shows that oxygen and hydrogen combine to form water.

v. 1. To carry out experiments.
Benjamin Franklin **experimented** with a kite to show that lightning was a form of electricity.

2. To try out new ideas or activities.
A good cook **experiments** with different herbs and spices to create new dishes.

flimsy
flim´ zē

adj. 1. Easily damaged or broken; not strongly made.
The cart was too **flimsy** to carry such a heavy load.

2. Not believable.
Saying you lost your pen is a **flimsy** excuse for not doing your homework.

heroic
hi rō´ ik

adj. 1. Very brave; showing great courage.
The teenager dove into the pond and made a **heroic** rescue of the child who couldn't swim.

2. Showing great determination; requiring enormous effort.
Firefighters made a **heroic** effort to put out the blaze.

lumber
lum´ bər

n. Wood that has been sawed into boards.
Have you ordered the **lumber** for the deck you are building?

v. To move in a clumsy or heavy way.
The old dog **lumbered** toward me.

Demonstrate for your partner how to lumber from one end of your table or desk to the other.

mimic
mim´ ik

v. 1. To copy or imitate closely.
The parrot fascinated us because it could **mimic** human speech so well.

2. To make fun of by imitating.
I got upset when you **mimicked** my friend's singing.

n. One who can imitate sounds, speech, or actions.
A good **mimic** carefully studies the person being imitated.

significant
sig nif´ ə kənt

adj. Important; full of meaning.
July 4, 1776, is a **significant** date in American history.

significance *n.* The quality of being important or of giving meaning.
The **significance** of the Bill of Rights is that it spells out important freedoms that should be enjoyed by all Americans.

Tell your partner the significance of friends in your life.

soar
sôr

v. 1. To fly high in the sky.
We watched the eagles **soar** until they were just specks in the sky.

2. To rise suddenly and rapidly.
The cost of a college education is expected to **soar** during the next few years.

| **spectator** | *n.* A person who watches an activity; an onlooker. |
| spek′ tāt ər | The **spectators** jostled each other as they rushed onto the field at the end of the game. |

suspend	*v.* 1. To hang while attached to something above.
sə spend′	The hammock was **suspended** from the porch ceiling.
	2. To stop for a while before going on.
	The subway **suspended** its main route for two days while the track was repaired.
	3. To bar from working, attending, or taking part for a while.
	The students caught cheating were **suspended** from school for one week.

Suspend your vocabulary study for thirty seconds while you take a deep breath.

| **terminate** | *v.* To bring or to come to an end. |
| tur′ mə nāt | Heavy rain **terminated** the tennis match after only ten minutes of play. |

Discuss with your partner what you plan to do when this school day is terminated.

| **unwieldy** | *adj.* Hard to handle or control because of large size or heaviness. |
| un wēl′ dē | The sofa was so **unwieldy** that getting it up three flights of stairs was a real challenge. |

9A Finding Meanings

Choose two phrases to form a sentence that correctly uses a word from Word List 9. Then write the sentence.

1. (a) If you suspend something,   (c) you bring it to an end.
   (b) you make a copy of it.   (d) If you terminate something,

   _____

   _____

2. (a) is easily broken.   (c) Something that is dense
   (b) is tightly packed.   (d) Something that is unwieldy

   _____

   _____

3. (a) To accomplish something
   (b) is to complete it successfully.
   (c) is to raise it to a higher level.
   (d) To mimic something

   _____

   _____

4. (a) that ends quickly.
   (b) A heroic effort is one
   (c) that shows great determination.
   (d) An absurd effort is one

   _____

   _____

5. (a) To ascend is to
   (b) To experiment is to
   (c) test or try out an idea.
   (d) increase in size or amount.

   _____

   _____

6. (a) A flimsy container is one that
   (b) An unwieldy container is
       one that
   (c) is not strongly made.
   (d) is meant to hold liquids.

   _____

   _____

7. (a) go to a higher level.
   (b) To ascend is to
   (c) fall into a drowsy state.
   (d) To lumber is to

   _____

   _____

8. (a) someone who plays.
   (b) someone who watches.
   (c) A spectator is
   (d) A mimic is

   _____

   _____

9. (a) move in a clumsy way.
   (b) To lumber is to
   (c) To soar is to
   (d) feel pain or discomfort.

   _____

   _____

10. (a) that is meaningful.   (c) An absurd statement is one
    (b) A significant statement is one   (d) that goes on longer than necessary.

_____

_____

Just the Right Word

Replace each phrase in bold with a single word (or form of the word) from the word list.

1. The movie is about the **very brave** women and men who fight forest fires.

2. The bicyclists could not see through the **very thick** fog.

3. The comedian usually gets lots of laughs when he **imitates the sound of** the voices of famous movie stars.

4. Francine's story about seeing a live dinosaur is **too silly to be believed.**

5. The *Mayflower* passengers' spirits **suddenly rose** when they got their first sight of land.

6. Leave the box where it is if you think it is too **large to be picked up and carried easily.**

7. Coach Louis told us that any player who fails a course will be **not allowed to take part in any games** for the rest of the season.

8. My family's visit to the Vietnam Veterans Memorial in Washington, D.C., was especially **full of meaning** because my uncle's name appears there.

9. The class's **carefully controlled attempt to discover if it was possible** to create a tiny volcano was very successful.

10. The **wood that has been sawed into boards** is stacked outside so that it will dry.

absurd
accomplish
ascend
dense
experiment
flimsy
heroic
lumber
mimic
significant
soar
spectator
suspend
terminate
unwieldy

9C Applying Meanings

Circle the letter or letters next to each correct answer. There may be more than one correct answer.

1. Which of the following can be **dense?**
   - (a) a person
   - (b) a crowd
   - (c) a hole
   - (d) a forest

2. Which of the following can **soar?**
   - (a) hopes
   - (b) cows
   - (c) prices
   - (d) birds

3. Which of the following would be an **accomplishment?**
   - (a) going to the kitchen
   - (b) winning a gold medal
   - (c) cheating on a test
   - (d) eating a pizza

4. Which of the following can be **suspended?**
   - (a) a bird feeder
   - (b) a mistake
   - (c) work
   - (d) a student

5. Which of the following would be **unwieldy?**
   - (a) a piano
   - (b) a flute
   - (c) a 72-inch television set
   - (d) a sleep sofa

6. Which of the following could have **significance?**
   - (a) a marriage
   - (b) a death
   - (c) a graduation
   - (d) a birth

7. Which of the following might you **experiment** with?
   - (a) hair styles
   - (b) a chemistry set
   - (c) clothing
   - (d) food

8. Which of the following can be **flimsy?**
   - (a) an aroma
   - (b) a task
   - (c) a shelter
   - (d) an excuse

9D Word Study: Homophones

Read the following sentences. If the word in bold is used correctly, write C on the line. If the word is used incorrectly, write I on the line.

Words that sound the same but have different meanings and/or spellings are called homophones. Here are five pairs of homophones:

prey/pray   course/coarse   route/root   hew/hue   soar/sore

1. We tried to get to the **route** of the problem. _____

2. The wolf seized its **prey** in its jaws. _____

3. I will **prey** for the safe return of those still missing. _____

4. The coastal **root** is the quickest way into town. _____

5. Mauricio's manners are rather **course.** _____

6. We watched the rocket **soar** until it was out of sight. _____

7. We **pray** that we will get there on time. _____

8. A **soar** knee kept me from racing. _____

9. We left the harbor and set a **coarse** for Nantucket. _____

10. The **route** to the mountain summit is well marked. _____

11. Sharp tools were needed to **hew** the boat from a single log. _____

12. My job was to **hue** the branches from the tree. _____

13. The cost of living is expected to **sore** in the coming year. _____

14. **Coarse** salt is made up of larger grains. _____

15. The daffodils were a deep yellow **hue.** _____

absurd
accomplish
ascend
dense
experiment
flimsy
heroic
lumber
mimic
significant
soar
spectator
suspend
terminate
unwieldy

The Sky's the Limit

For as long as people have watched birds **soar** far above the earth, they have dreamed of being able to fly. The Montgolfier brothers of France, Jacques and Joseph, thought of a way this might be possible. In 1782, after observing smoke and hot air rising from a fire, they made a small cloth balloon and filled it with hot air. Then they watched it rise seventy feet. Hot air is less **dense** than cold air. This means that hot air is lighter. The warmer, lighter air inside the balloon caused it to rise.

The next year they built a balloon with a diameter of thirty-five feet. They filled this one with hot air also; they burned wool and straw on an iron grate that rested in a large basket **suspended** beneath the balloon. This one rose successfully, too. So, they built another balloon that was even bigger. In September 1783, the Montgolfier brothers gathered a large crowd, which included the French royal family. The brothers placed a sheep, a duck, and a rooster in the balloon's basket and released it. The balloon **ascended** to a height of fifteen hundred feet. It stayed in the air for eight minutes.

A hot-air balloon rises because it is lighter than the air around it. But the idea that something heavier than air could ever get off the ground seemed **absurd** to most people. Not everyone thought so, however. By the late 1800s, after the invention of the steam engine and, later on, the much lighter gasoline engine, the first airplanes were being made. Some of these had movable wings to **mimic** the flapping of birds' wings. These were too **unwieldy** to fly. Some were powered by steam engines. These were so heavy they couldn't get off the ground. When the airplane's frame was made lighter, the plane became **flimsy.** This was another big problem. Indeed, many early flights **terminated** in a crash. Some people believed that to fly in those days was almost a **heroic** act.

It took another pair of brothers, Orville and Wilbur Wright, to figure out how to build a machine that could stay up in the air. The Wright brothers made and repaired bicycles for a living at their shop in Dayton, Ohio. They were like many other people at the time; the idea of flying fascinated them. They spent some time **experimenting** with kites and gliders. Then they built a plane with rigid wings that was powered by a small gasoline engine. This was much lighter than a steam engine.

December 17, 1903, is a **significant** date in the history of flying. On that day in Kitty Hawk, North Carolina, the Wright brothers demonstrated that a heavier-than-air machine could successfully fly. Just a handful of **spectators** were there to watch. The plane, with Orville Wright at the controls, began to **lumber** across the grassy field. The people cheered as they saw the plane lift off the ground. It stayed in the air for twelve seconds before landing about 120 feet away.

That afternoon the Wright brothers made three more flights— the longest, lasting fifty-nine seconds, covered 852 feet. They had **accomplished** their goal. They had made it possible for humans to fulfill their dreams of flight. One hundred years later, an exact copy of the Wright brothers' plane was built. To celebrate the one hundredth birthday of their achievement, it was supposed to make a flight in Kitty Hawk on December 17, 2003. It looked just like the Wright brothers' plane, but sadly it failed to get off the ground. You can see the airplane the Wright brothers built at the National Air and Space Museum in Washington, D.C.

▶ **Answer each of the following questions with a sentence. If a question does not contain a vocabulary word from the lesson's word list, use one in your answer. Use each word only once.**

| absurd |
| accomplish |
| ascend |
| dense |
| experiment |
| flimsy |
| heroic |
| lumber |
| mimic |
| significant |
| soar |
| spectator |
| suspend |
| terminate |
| unwieldy |

1. Why is a hot-air balloon able to rise?

_____

_____

2. Why is Kitty Hawk, North Carolina, **significant** in the history of flying?

_____

_____

3. Describe one **accomplishment** of the Montgolfier brothers.

_____

_____

4. How high did the Montgolfier brothers' first balloon rise in 1782?

_____

_____

5. Why were the early airplanes with flapping wings unsuccessful?

_____

_____

6. What is the meaning of **soar** as it is used in the passage?

_____

_____

7. What important family saw the Montgolfiers' hot-air balloon in September 1783?

_____

_____

8. What is the meaning of **suspended** as it is used in the passage?

_____

_____

9. Why were injuries probably a common occurrence among the first fliers?

_____

_____

10. Why did some early planes have movable wings?

_____

_____

11. How did the Wright brothers test their ideas before building the first airplane?

_____

_____

12. What is the meaning of **lumber** as it is used in the passage?

_____

_____

13. What problem developed when airplane frames were made lighter?

_____

_____

14. What might an aircraft designer today think of the idea of using a steam engine to power an airplane?

_____

_____

15. Why is it not considered **heroic** to fly in today's airplanes?

_____

_____

absurd

accomplish

ascend

dense

experiment

flimsy

heroic

lumber

mimic

significant

soar

spectator

suspend

terminate

unwieldy

Fun & Fascinating FACTS

- The noun formed from **ascend** is *ascent*, the act of rising or going higher. (Our *ascent* to the summit took four hours.) The antonyms of these words are *descend* and *descent*. Don't confuse *ascent* with its homophone *assent*. *Assent* means "agreement." (We cannot give our *assent* to the project until these changes are made.)

- **Soar** and *sore* are also homophones. A *sore* is a painful spot on the body, often with the skin broken. *Sore* is also an *adjective* and means "painful."

- A *pendant* is something that hangs from a chain around a person's neck. This word comes from the Latin *pendere,* which means "to hang." **Suspend** comes from the same Latin root.

- **Spectator** is formed from the Latin *spectare,* which means "to see" or "to look at." Two other words formed from this root are *inspect* and *spectacles*. When you *inspect* something, you look at it closely; *spectacles*, another word for *eyeglasses*, help a person see better.

- The Latin *terminus* means "end." It provides the root for the verb **terminate.** Several other words are formed from this root. A *terminus* is the end of a bus or train line. *Terminal* means "of or relating to an end." A *terminal* illness is one that ends in death. Something that is *interminable* seems to go on without an end. (After an *interminable* wait, we finally saw the doctor.)

terminate

verb To end.

Word Family

terminated (verb)
terminating (verb)
termination (noun)

Synonyms and Antonyms

Synonyms: conclude, end, finish
Antonyms: begin, open, start

Discussion & Writing Prompt

Describe how you would **terminate** a computer game or computer program.

2 min.	3 min.
1. Turn and talk to your partner or group.	**2.** Write 2–4 sentences.
Use this space to take notes or draw your ideas.	Be ready to share what you have written.

Lesson 10

Word List

Study the definitions of the words. Then do the exercises that follow.

available ə vāl´ ə bəl 	*adj.* Easy to get; present and ready for use. The salesperson said the jacket was **available** in black, brown, and white. .... *Chat with your partner about the kinds of transportation that are available in your area.*
bondage bän´ dij	*n.* The state of being enslaved. It is shocking that some people still live in **bondage** in the twenty-first century.
donate dō´ nāt	*v.* To give to those in need, often through an organization. People across the country **donated** food and clothing to the victims of the flood. **donation** *n.* Whatever is donated, such as money or goods. **Donations** to help rebuild the community center now total sixty thousand dollars.
establish e stab´ lish	*v.* 1. To set up or begin. **Established** in 1636, Harvard College, now part of Harvard University, is the oldest college in the United States. 2. To show to be true. Scientists have **established** beyond any doubt that smoking causes cancer and other diseases. **establishment** *n.* Something that has been established, especially a place of business or a public building. Many restaurants, stores, and other **establishments** are open all night. .... *Discuss with your partner whether it is established that good grades will mean success in life.*
evade ē vād´	*v.* 1. To keep away from; to avoid being caught. The chipmunk **evaded** the cat by scrambling up a tree. 2. To avoid doing or answering. People who **evade** their responsibilities usually end up wishing they hadn't. **evasive** *adj.* Carefully avoiding saying too much; not open or direct. The teenagers were **evasive** when asked where they had been all evening.

| **liberate**
lib′ ər āt | *v.* To free.
A group objecting to trapping animals opened the monkey cages and **liberated** the animals inside them. |

Talk to your partner about what would happen if all the animals at the zoo were liberated.

| **numerous**
noo′ mər əs | *adj.* A large number; very many.
The bus makes **numerous** stops before it leaves us at school. |

| **occasion**
ō kā′ zhən | *n.* 1. A particular time.
I recognized Ranesha at once because we had met on a previous **occasion**.

2. A special event.
My grandparents' anniversary party was a fun **occasion** for the whole family.

occasional *adj.* Happening once in a while.
We make an **occasional** trip to town to pick up supplies. |

| **oppose**
ə pōz′ | *v.* To be or act against.
Moin, my best friend, will **oppose** me in the chess tournament.

opposition *n.* (äp ə zish′ ən) The act or condition of being against.
There was no **opposition** to the suggested plan, which passed by a vote of 16 to 0. |

| **prohibit**
prō hib′ it | *v.* To forbid by law or order.
The law now **prohibits** smoking in many public places. |

Tell your partner an activity you think should be prohibited on the school playground.

| **pursue**
pər soo′ | *v.* 1. To follow in order to capture; to chase.
Police **pursued** the stolen car in a high-speed chase across town.

2. To seek actively; to carry on with.
Do you intend to **pursue** a career in medicine?

pursuit *n.* 1. The act of following after.
In the early 1930s, people desperate for work poured into cities in **pursuit** of jobs.

2. An activity, as a job or sport, that a person takes part in.
Jennie and Ahmed enjoy canoeing and other outdoor **pursuits** during the summer. |

Talk with your partner about your favorite indoor pursuit, such as video games or reading.

reassure
rē ə shoor´

v. To make less worried or fearful; to comfort.
I was nervous before the recital, but my piano teacher **reassured** me.

reassurance *n.* The act of giving comfort or the state of receiving comfort.
Coach Ward's **reassurances** made us more optimistic about our chances of winning.

reluctant
rē luk´ tənt

adj. Not wanting to do something; unwilling.
We were **reluctant** to leave our warm beds when we saw the ice on the windows.

reluctance *n.* The state of not wanting to do something.
With great **reluctance,** I agreed to clean my room before my cousins arrived on Saturday.

Tell your partner about an activity you are reluctant to try because you are afraid you might fail, like learning to play an instrument or trying out for a team.

superior
sə pir´ ē ər

adj. 1. Excellent of its kind.
Margot made the team because she is a **superior** runner.

2. Higher in position or rank.
A general is **superior** to a sergeant in the army.

n. A person of higher rank.
I reported to my **superior** as soon as I returned to work.

Discuss with your partner what person is superior to your teacher at school.

yearn
yʉrn

v. To want very badly; to be filled with longing.
Dorothy told the Wizard of Oz that she **yearned** to be back in Kansas.

yearning *n.* A longing or strong desire.
As rain leaked slowly through the roof of our tent, I was filled with a **yearning** for my warm, dry bed at home.

10A

Using Words in Context

Read the following sentences. If the word in bold is used correctly, write C on the line. If the word is used incorrectly, write I on the line.

1. (a) The **donation** said I was hired and asked when I could start. _____
   (b) I **donated** ten dollars to the Animal Welfare Fund. _____
   (c) People can **donate** blood if they choose to. _____
   (d) The man's **donations** thumped in his chest. _____

2. (a) People who **evade** doing their homework may find themselves in trouble. _____
   (b) Tiger ants are **evading** the country through the south. _____
   (c) The prey must stay alert at all times to **evade** the hunter. _____
   (d) Wanda was **evasive** when her mother asked where she'd been. _____

3. (a) The trophy is **prohibited** with the name of the winner. _____
   (b) Campfires are **prohibited** when the weather is very dry. _____
   (c) The rainbow **prohibited** a rush of people to the window. _____
   (d) Eating is **prohibited** in the classroom. _____

4. (a) I was **reluctant** to enter because I was afraid of what I'd find. _____
   (b) I earn **reluctance** from my parents for doing the dishes every night. _____
   (c) Nadine showed some **reluctance** when she was asked to talk in front of the crowd. _____
   (d) The weather here is too **reluctant** for snow. _____

5. (a) Soldiers should salute their **superior** officers. _____
   (b) Some believe cheddar cheese is **superior** to Swiss cheese. _____
   (c) There are hidden chambers in the Great Pyramid's **superior**. _____
   (d) The earth's **superior** is a core of molten iron. _____

6. (a) Eva grabbed her **pursuit** and took out some money. _____
   (b) One of the **pursuits** Tasha enjoys is jogging. _____
   (c) Purple is my favorite **pursuit**. _____
   (d) We were in **pursuit** of the cute rabbit when it ducked under a fence and disappeared. _____

7. (a) I visit my aunt in Sacramento **occasionally.** _____
   (b) Your birthday is an **occasion** to celebrate. _____
   (c) We met three times, and on each **occasion** he ignored me. _____
   (d) My favorite **occasion** is the baseball diamond. _____

8. (a) There was no **opposition** to the students' request for a baseball club. _____
   (b) He said I owed him money, but actually the **opposition** was true. _____
   (c) Judah will **oppose** Shakir in the tennis final. _____
   (d) I **oppose** to stay in New York before leaving for Miami. _____

9. (a) There are **numerous** stars in the night sky. _____
   (b) We started to feel **numerous** as the temperature dropped. _____
   (c) See a doctor right away if the wound starts to get **numerous.** _____
   (d) The orange leaves on the tree are starting to become more **numerous.** _____

10. (a) My favorite old **establishment** in town is the drive-in movie theater. _____
    (b) The U.S. Marine Corps was **established** in 1798. _____
    (c) The study **established** that texting is the main cause of car accidents. _____
    (d) The girl **established** her best friend and then went into the house. _____

available
bondage
donate
establish
evade
liberate
numerous
occasion
oppose
prohibit
pursue
reassure
reluctant
superior
yearn

10B Making Connections

Circle the letter next to each correct answer. There may be more than one correct answer.

1. Which word or words go with *slavery?*
   (a) bondage   (b) liberate   (c) victim   (d) donation

2. Which word or words go with *ready for something?*
   (a) occasional   (b) reluctant   (c) evasive   (d) available

3. Which word or words go with *once in a while?*
   (a) eventually   (b) occasionally   (c) numerously   (d) desperately

4. Which word or words go with *not serious?*
   (a) foolhardy   (b) absurd   (c) frivolous   (d) occasional

5. Which word or words go with *begin?*
   (a) evade   (b) donation   (c) launch   (d) establish

6. Which word or words go with *want a lot?*
   (a) establish   (b) desire   (c) occasion   (d) yearn

7. Which word or words go with *comfort?*
   (a) establish   (b) embrace   (c) prohibit   (d) reassure

8. Which word or words go with *better than most?*
   (a) superior   (b) numerous   (c) exceptional   (d) reluctant

9. Which word or words go with *give?*
   (a) evade   (b) prohibit   (c) donate   (d) assemble

10. Which word or words go with *not allowed?*
   (a) pursued   (b) prohibited   (c) banned   (d) liberated

10c Determining Meanings

Circle the letter next to each answer choice that correctly completes the sentence. There may be more than one correct answer.

1. We **evaded**
   (a) her parents and got inside quickly.
   (b) our way through the maze in record time.
   (c) ourselves into thinking we were safe.
   (d) their questions by changing the subject.

2. The **opposition**
   (a) to the new gym is growing every day.
   (b) of the word *up* is the word *down*.
   (c) of each bus is yellow with black stripes.
   (d) wanted more homework and fewer quizzes, unlike the rest of us.

3. He **pursued**
   (a) the opposing team's player to the goal line with ten seconds left in the game.
   (b) every goal he thought he could achieve.
   (c) gravity as it held Earth in the sun's orbit.
   (d) pasta topped with sauce and served with bread.

4. We **liberated**
   (a) the caged bird by leaving the door open.
   (b) ourselves a cold beverage from the refrigerator.
   (c) ourselves by taking off our coats and running in the snow.
   (d) the question very carefully before deciding.

5. The **yearning**
   (a) was sold to a farm when it was old enough to be ridden.
   (b) to escape was all Evangeline thought about.
   (c) to learn more is what kept Albert Einstein working.
   (d) was part of the cargo being loaded at the dock.

6. I **reluctantly**
   (a) lent my catcher's mitt to my friend who always loses things.
   (b) stepped into the darkness, keeping my flashlight handy.
   (c) always love swimming with the dolphins.
   (d) get good grades because I like to study every night.

| available |
| bondage |
| donate |
| establish |
| evade |
| liberate |
| numerous |
| occasion |
| oppose |
| prohibit |
| pursue |
| reassure |
| reluctant |
| superior |
| yearn |

7. The rules **prohibited**

    (a) skateboarding in the park.

    (b) fishing from the pier.

    (c) what was allowed.

    (d) spectators from going onto the track.

8. We were **reassured**

    (a) when our friend kept his promise.

    (b) down the hall.

    (c) a glass of water.

    (d) that everything was being done to make us comfortable.

10D Completing Sentences

Complete the sentences to demonstrate your knowledge of the words in bold.

1. A special **occasion** for me is

    _____.

2. I **yearn** for

    _____.

3. I would be **reluctant** to

    _____.

4. When I have some extra money, I will make a **donation** to

    _____.

5. I wish I could **establish** a national holiday to

    _____.

6. I should respect my **superiors** because

    _____.

7. One thing I would **oppose** is

    _____.

8. One activity I'd like to **pursue** is

    _____.

9. An example of something that is **numerous** is

_____ .

10. If someone is held in **bondage,** it means that person is

_____ .

10E Vocabulary in Context

Read the passage.

With Moses to the Promised Land

Harriet Tubman was born enslaved in Maryland in 1820. From the time she was a young child, she **yearned** to be free. The hard physical work that she was forced to do made her very strong. And though as an enslaved person she received no education, she was also intelligent and quick-thinking. She put these qualities to good use, first in making her own escape and later in helping others to do the same.

When Harriet was in her late twenties, the slave owner she was forced to work for died. She feared she would be sold and sent to the deep South. There the work was harder and slave owners more cruel. She decided to escape instead. She urged her brothers to come with her on the journey north. They **reluctantly** joined her. Soon after they set out, though, her brothers turned back. They were afraid of being caught. So Harriet continued alone, traveling mostly at night. Eventually she made it safely to Philadelphia. Although she had found freedom, she couldn't enjoy it; so many others, including her family, were still living in **bondage.**

In 1850, Congress passed a law making it a crime to help runaway enslaved people. But over the next eleven years, Harriet returned **numerous** times to the South to lead other enslaved people to Canada. In Canada, slavery was **prohibited** and people who had escaped slavery were welcome. Altogether during this time she helped to **liberate** over three hundred people. That number included her parents and brothers and sisters. Along the way she stayed with people who offered food and shelter in their homes, often at great risk to themselves. These houses were called "stations" on what became known as the Underground Railroad.

available
bondage
donate
establish
evade
liberate
numerous
occasion
oppose
prohibit
pursue
reassure
reluctant
superior
yearn

Between trips, Harriet took whatever jobs were **available**—cooking, sewing, or cleaning. She used some of her money to help formerly enslaved people start new lives. She always saved some of it for her next journey south. She had many friends who **opposed** slavery; when she needed money for her work, they would help her by making **donations.**

Slave owners were furious at having their "property" stolen. They offered as much as forty thousand dollars for Harriet Tubman's capture. She was often **pursued** by people who wanted the reward. She had many narrow escapes, but she always managed to **evade** being caught. The enslaved people she helped called her Moses because she led them to freedom, just as Moses had led the Jewish people out of slavery in Egypt thousands of years earlier.

During the Civil War, Harriet Tubman worked for the North as a nurse in the Union army. Enslaved people had been taught by slave owners to be afraid of the Union soldiers. But Harriet went behind enemy lines and was able to **reassure** them. They believed her when she told them they had nothing to fear from the Union army. On some **occasions** while there, she acted as a spy, reporting to her **superiors** when she returned to the Union side. After the war she worked energetically to start schools in the South for freed people, even though she herself could not read or write. She eventually settled in Auburn, New York, where she **established** a nursing home for elderly African Americans. When she died in 1913, thousands mourned this courageous woman who had helped so many people.

▶ **Answer each of the following questions with a sentence. If a question does not contain a vocabulary word from the lesson's word list, use one in your answer. Use each word only once.**

1. What did the law that Congress passed in 1850 **prohibit?**

_____

_____

2. What is the meaning of the word **superiors** as it is used in the passage?

_____

_____

3. How did Harriet Tubman feel about being enslaved?

_____

_____

4. Why were her brothers **reluctant** to go with Tubman?

_____

_____

5. How did Harriet Tubman's friends help her?

_____

_____

6. What is the meaning of **evade** as it is used in the passage?

_____

_____

7. Why was Harriet Tubman called Moses by those she helped?

_____

_____

8. How do you think Tubman might have **reassured** the enslaved people she was helping?

_____

_____

9. In what way did the stations on the Underground Railroad help **liberate** the enslaved people?

_____

_____

10. Why do you think some people opened their homes to escaping enslaved people?

_____

_____

11. How did the reward for her capture affect Tubman's later trips to the South?

_____

_____

12. What is the meaning of **established** as it is used in the passage?

_____

_____

available
bondage
donate
establish
evade
liberate
numerous
occasion
oppose
prohibit
pursue
reassure
reluctant
superior
yearn

13. Why do you think most enslaved people were unable to read or write?

_____

_____

14. What two activities did Tubman engage in during the Civil War?

_____

_____

15. Why do you think Tubman made **numerous** trips south even though it was very dangerous for her?

_____

_____

Fun & Fascinating FACTS

- The Statue of *Liberty* is a symbol of freedom to people all over the world. To hand out money *liberally* is to hand it out freely, without exercising very much control. Both these words, together with **liberate,** are formed from the Latin *liber,* which means "free." It's interesting to note that the Latin word for "book" is also *liber.* (A *library* is a place where *books* are kept.) There is a clear connection between books and freedom. A person who cannot read a book is in a kind of prison; learning to read sets the mind free to explore the world and everything in it.

- The noun formed from the verb **prohibit** is *prohibition,* an order to stop or the act of forbidding. The word is associated with a fascinating period in United States history. In 1919, the Eighteenth Amendment to the Constitution prohibited the sale of alcoholic beverages. The result was that many citizens ignored the law, and gangsters such as Al Capone grew rich by illegally selling alcoholic beverages. Within a few years it was clear that the amendment had failed. Prohibition, as this time was known, ended in 1933 when the Twenty-First Amendment was added to the Constitution. This one abolished the Eighteenth.

establish

verb 1. To set up or begin.

2. To find out facts that show something to be true.

Word Family
established (adjective)
establishment (noun)

Context Clues
These sentences give clues to the meaning of **establish.**

*The principal wants to **establish** an after-school music program.*

*Space scientists are trying to **establish** if there is water on Mars.*

Discussion & Writing Prompt

Imagine you are **establishing** a new club at school. What kind of club would you **establish,** and why?

2 min.	3 min.
1. Turn and talk to your partner or group.	2. Write 2–4 sentences.
Use this space to take notes or draw your ideas.	Be ready to share what you have written.

Study the definitions of the words. Then do the exercises that follow.

accelerate
ak sel´ ər āt

v. 1. To go or to cause to go faster.
The morning train quickly **accelerates** once it leaves the station.

2. To bring about at an earlier time.
Increased sunlight **accelerates** the growth of plants.

altitude
al´ tə tood

n. Height above sea level or the earth's surface.
Mexico City lies at an **altitude** of almost 8,000 feet.

anxious
aŋk´ shəs

adj. 1. Worried; concerned.
I am **anxious** about how I did on the Spanish test.

2. Eager; wishing strongly.
After writing to each other for over a year, the two penpals are **anxious** to meet.

anxiety *n.* (aŋ zī´ ə tē) Great uneasiness or concern.
Our **anxiety** grew as the day of the big test approached.

brace
brās

v. 1. To make stronger by giving support to.
Mom **braced** the table leg with a metal strip to keep it from wobbling.

2. To make ready for a shock; to prepare.
After the bus driver's warning, I grabbed the pole and **braced** myself for a bump.

n. Something used to support a weak part.
I wore a **brace** on my leg for four weeks after I injured it doing a high jump.

bracing *adj.* Giving energy to; refreshing.
After spending most of the summer in the city, we found the cool mountain air wonderfully **bracing.**

Share with your partner a time when you braced yourself because you thought something bad was going to happen.

confident
kän´ fi dent

adj. Certain; sure.
We are **confident** we will win Saturday's hockey game.

confidence *n.* 1. A lack of doubt; a feeling of being certain.
My parents showed their **confidence** in me by letting me repair the car by myself.

2. Trust in another to keep a secret.
Because Felix told me this in **confidence,** I cannot answer your question.

Tell your partner how you would feel if you told someone a secret in confidence, and then that person told your secret to others.

---

contact
kän´ takt

n. 1. The touching or joining of two things.
Contact with a live wire will give you an electric shock.

2. The condition of being in communication with others.
Before the telephone was invented, people usually stayed in **contact** by writing letters.

v. To communicate with.
The Apollo astronauts could not **contact** Earth while their spaceship was traveling behind the moon.

Talk to your partner about what happens if poison ivy contacts your skin.

---

exult
eg zult´

v. To be joyful; to show great happiness.
Senator Gray's supporters **exulted** when she easily won reelection.

exultant *adj.* Very happy.
Theresa was **exultant** when she crossed the 10K finish line first.

---

hangar
haŋ´ ər

n. A building where aircraft are kept and repaired.
The pilot steered the plane out of the **hangar** and onto the runway.

---

maximum
maks´ i məm

n. The greatest or highest number or amount.
The largest bus we have for school trips holds a **maximum** of fifty people.

adj. Being the greatest or highest number or amount.
The **maximum** speed of this car is eighty miles per hour.

Discuss with your partner the maximum number of times you might be able to sink a free throw in ten minutes.

---

methodical
mə thäd´ i kəl

adj. Done in a regular, orderly way.
Our **methodical** search of the house failed to turn up any evidence of the lost key.

nonchalant
nän shə länt´

adj. Having the appearance of not caring; seeming to show a lack of concern.
Your **nonchalant** attitude to schoolwork worries your parents.

proceed
prō sēd´

v. To go on, especially after stopping for a while; to continue.
The subway train **proceeded** on its way after I got off at 14th Street.

Stop talking to your partner for fifteen seconds and then proceed with your work on this lesson.

saunter
sôn´ tər

v. To walk without hurrying; to stroll in a relaxed, unhurried manner.
Pedestrians **saunter** along the river bank, enjoying the afternoon sunshine.

n. A relaxed, unhurried walk.
Our **saunter** around the park was abruptly terminated by a violent thunderstorm.

solo
sō´ lō

n. A musical piece for one voice or a single instrument.
The long guitar **solo** was the best part of the rock concert.

adj. Made or done by one person.
I told my mom I would do a **solo** cleaning of the kitchen, so she could take a break.

v. To fly alone, especially for the first time.
Most student pilots **solo** after ten hours of lessons.

Talk to your partner about where you would like to go on a solo trip when you are older.

stall
stôl

n. 1. A place for an animal in a barn.
Each horse in the barn had its own **stall.**

2. A small stand or booth where things are sold.
I purchased this pottery at one of the **stalls** at the county fair.

v. 1. To suddenly lose power.
He will **stall** the engine if he doesn't give the car some gas.

2. To delay by being evasive.
I tried to **stall** the teacher by saying I had lost my book.

Tell your partner about your favorite food stall at a carnival, fair, or festival.

Finding Meanings

Choose two phrases to form a sentence that correctly uses a word from Word List 11. Then write the sentence.

1. (a) A plane's hangar is
   (b) the amount of cargo it carries.
   (c) its height above sea level.
   (d) A plane's altitude is

   _____

   _____

2. (a) To accelerate an engine is to
   (b) cause it to lose power suddenly.
   (c) run it at its lowest speed.
   (d) To stall an engine is to

   _____

   _____

3. (a) a performance by one person.
   (b) A saunter is
   (c) A solo is
   (d) a support for a broken part.

   _____

   _____

4. (a) a place where goods are sold.
   (b) a place where planes are kept.
   (c) A brace is
   (d) A hangar is

   _____

   _____

5. (a) stop suddenly.
   (b) To accelerate is to
   (c) go faster.
   (d) To exult is to

   _____

   _____

6. (a) does things in an orderly way.
   (b) is filled with happiness.
   (c) An anxious person
   (d) A methodical person

   _____

   _____

7. (a) A contact is
   (b) A brace is
   (c) a support for a broken part.
   (d) a place where business is done.

   _____

   _____

accelerate
altitude
anxious
brace
confident
contact
exult
hangar
maximum
methodical
nonchalant
proceed
saunter
solo
stall

8. (a) To be nonchalant about something is
   (b) To be anxious about something is
   (c) to be concerned about it.
   (d) to be very happy about it.

_____

_____

9. (a) To be confident is to be
   (b) sure of oneself.
   (c) reluctant to act or speak.
   (d) To be exultant is to be

_____

_____

10. (a) walk in a relaxed, unhurried manner.
    (b) show a willingness to help.
    (c) To saunter is to
    (d) To proceed is to

_____

_____

11B Just the Right Word

Replace each phrase in bold with a single word (or form of the word) from the word list.

1. Five striped bass is the **greatest number** you are allowed to catch this month.

2. After hanging up our coats, we will **make our way** to our seats in the nice restaurant.

3. Baseball fans are **filled with happiness** when their favorite team makes it to the World Series.

4. I plan to fly a plane **without my instructor** tomorrow.

5. The breeze off the ocean is very **refreshing and gives one renewed energy.**

6. The trainer led the horse back to its **enclosed place in the stable** after her ride.

7. I lost **the possibility to communicate** with my friends after they moved out of state.

8. The skiers were **showing no concern** as they started down the steep slope.

9. Jayesh was up at dawn, **very eager** to be on his way.

10. I am telling you what the teacher told me in **the expectation that you will keep it a secret.**

11c Applying Meanings

Circle the letter or letters next to each correct answer. There may be more than one correct answer.

1. Which of the following are measurements of **altitude?**
   - (a) three tons
   - (b) twenty dollars
   - (c) six miles
   - (d) ten thousand feet

2. Which of the following might you find in a **hangar?**
   - (a) airplanes
   - (b) spare parts
   - (c) tools
   - (d) horses

3. Which of the following might cause a person to **exult?**
   - (a) receiving a scholarship
   - (b) being liberated
   - (c) an exceptional harvest
   - (d) being thrown into bondage

4. Which of the following remarks shows **confidence?**
   - (a) "I give up."
   - (b) "I can do it."
   - (c) "I'm not sure."
   - (d) "Let me show you how."

5. Which of the following can be **accelerated?**
   - (a) plant growth
   - (b) an automobile
   - (c) a route
   - (d) a crevice

accelerate
altitude
anxious
brace
confident
contact
exult
hangar
maximum
methodical
nonchalant
proceed
saunter
solo
stall

6. Which of the following might cause **anxiety?**
   (a) becoming ill   (c) being denounced
   (b) losing a job   (d) finding a wallet

7. Which of the following can **stall?**
   (a) a horse   (c) an airplane
   (b) an engine   (d) a person

8. Which of the following could be used as a **brace?**
   (a) a steel rod   (c) a length of string
   (b) a broom handle   (d) a handkerchief

Word Study: Prefixes

Complete the words by providing the correct form of the prefix.

The prefix *com-* means "with." To *com*plain about something is to find fault *with* it. To make certain words easier to say, this prefix is sometimes written *con-*.

1. _____nect   to put together with

2. _____sume   to do away with or destroy

3. _____fident   pleased or satisfied with oneself

4. _____bine   to put one thing with another

5. _____patible   getting along with another

6. _____versation   a talk with someone

7. _____tent   satisfied with what one has

8. _____prehend   to understand or be familiar with

9. _____tact   get in touch with

10. _____panion   someone who travels with another

Vocabulary in Context
Read the passage.

Off You Go into the Wild Blue Yonder

After ten weeks of flying lessons, which is about the average instruction period, you are ready to take your first **solo** flight. Today, your instructor will be on the ground instead of sitting beside you. When you arrive at the airfield, you see her standing outside the **hangar,** and she greets you with a friendly wave. As the two of you chat, you try to sound as **nonchalant** as possible, even though your heart is pounding. She must see how nervous you are because she remarks that she has complete **confidence** in you. That makes you feel better, and you begin to relax a little as the two of you **saunter** over to the plane.

After climbing inside and taking a deep breath, you **methodically** complete the checklist of the plane's controls. Then, you wait for a signal from the control tower to **proceed.** As soon as it comes, your feelings of **anxiety** leave you. You start the engine and release the brake. You open the throttle a little, feeding more gasoline to the engine and causing the propeller to whirl faster. The plane starts to move forward. You taxi onto the runway, facing into the wind, and wait.

A voice from the control tower comes through your headphones, giving you permission to take off. You open the throttle wide, and the plane **accelerates** down the runway. Your right hand rests on the "stick," a control that lifts the plane's nose when pulled back and drops the nose when pushed forward. The plane is now traveling so fast that you can feel it trying to leave the ground. You pull back gently on the stick. The ground suddenly drops away beneath you. You are flying!

You have been told to go no faster than eighty-five miles an hour, although the plane has a **maximum** speed of twice that. You reach an **altitude** of five hundred feet and ease back on the throttle, watching your air speed carefully. If it drops below fifty-five miles an hour, the plane will **stall.** To increase speed, you push the stick forward, dropping the nose slightly. Already, it is time to make the first turn. You push the stick gently to the left, and the wing on that side drops, causing the plane to make a turn, or "bank" as you have learned to call it. There are so many things to think about that you hardly notice the view. After making three more left banks, you are on your final approach.

accelerate

altitude

anxious

brace

confident

contact

exult

hangar

maximum

methodical

nonchalant

proceed

saunter

solo

stall

The control tower clears you for landing. You reduce the amount that the throttle is open and can feel the plane dropping. Not too fast. Not too steep an angle. Come in too high and you'll overshoot the runway; come in too low, and you'll fall short. You **brace** yourself as the runway comes rushing toward you.

When the plane is just inches off the ground, you close the throttle and pull back on the stick to raise the nose. Without power from the engine, the wings no longer support the plane, and it drops. You don't want to be too high when this happens or the plane will bounce as it makes **contact** with the ground. But you make a perfect landing. An **exultant** feeling sweeps over you as you roll down the runway and come to a stop. Flying is fun!

▶ **Answer each of the following questions with a sentence. If a question does not contain a vocabulary word from the lesson's word list, use one in your answer. Use each word only once.**

1. What large airport building would be easily seen from the air?

   _____

   _____

2. What is the **maximum** speed allowed on the flight?

   _____

   _____

3. What is the meaning of **stall** as it is used in the passage?

   _____

   _____

4. What might happen if the check of the controls before a flight is less than **methodical?**

   _____

   _____

5. How does the pilot receive instructions when in the plane?

   _____

   _____

6. What is the meaning of **confidence** as it is used in the passage?

_____

_____

7. How does the pilot try to hide a feeling of nervousness before the flight?

_____

_____

8. How is it made clear that the pilot didn't hurry over to the plane?

_____

_____

9. What does the pilot need before **proceeding** to take off?

_____

_____

10. How much instruction is usually necessary before one is allowed to fly alone?

_____

_____

11. What happens to the plane's air speed when the throttle is opened wide?

_____

_____

12. What happens to the plane when the pilot closes the throttle?

_____

_____

13. What is the meaning of **brace** as it is used in the passage?

_____

_____

14. How might the pilot **exult** after landing safely?

_____

_____

accelerate
altitude
anxious
brace
confident
contact
exult
hangar
maximum
methodical
nonchalant
proceed
saunter
solo
stall

15. How might you feel if you were a pilot making your first flight alone?

_____

_____

Fun & Fascinating FACTS

- A plane's **altitude** is measured by an instrument called an *altimeter,* which shows the height above sea level, not the distance to the ground below. It does this by measuring the density of the air outside. If the **altitude** of a plane that is flying over the ocean is five thousand feet, that means the plane is literally five thousand feet high in the air. But if the plane is flying over land that is 4,900 feet above sea level, the **altitude** of the plane is still measured as five thousand feet. In the second case, the plane would actually be just barely skimming the ground.

- Don't confuse **hangar,** a large building where aircraft are kept, with *hanger,* a metal, wood, or plastic frame on which clothes are hung. These two words are homophones.

- The opposite of **maximum** is *minimum.* (For many years, most highways in the United States had a *maximum* speed of 55 m.p.h. and a *minimum* speed of 40 m.p.h.)

- In Lesson 7, you learned several words formed from the Latin *solus,* which means "alone; without company." **Solo** is another of those words. A *solo* is an activity, musical or otherwise, performed by one person. A piece of music for two people is called a *duet;* for three people, a *trio;* and for four people, a *quartet.*

Vocabulary **E**xtension

contact

noun 1. Communication with someone else.

2. When two or more people or things touch each other.

verb To communicate with.

Context Clues

These sentences give clues to the meaning of **contact.**

> *Paula and Ricardo have weekly **contact** on the phone with their favorite aunt.*

> *When vinegar and baking soda come into **contact** with each other, the result is a fizzy mess.*

> *Louise **contacted** her teacher by e-mail to ask about the assignment.*

Discussion & Writing Prompt

Write a list of as many different ways you can think of to keep in **contact** with someone.

2 min.	3 min.
1. Turn and talk to your partner or group.	**2.** Write 2–4 sentences.
Use this space to take notes or draw your ideas.	Be ready to share what you have written.

Word List

Study the definitions of the words. Then do the exercises that follow.

convalesce
kän və les´

v. To get back health and strength after an illness.
After the operation on my knee, I will **convalesce** at home.

dedicate
ded´ i kāt

v. 1. To set aside for a certain purpose.
My parents **dedicate** part of their income to saving for my college education.

2. To devote to a serious purpose.
Madame Curie **dedicated** her life to science.

3. To name, address, or set aside as an honor.
The authors **dedicated** the book to their two children.

Discuss with your partner an important issue you might dedicate your life to and why.

dictate
dik´ tāt

v. 1. To give orders; to command.
The law **dictates** that children attend school until they are sixteen.

2. To say aloud while another writes down the words.
I **dictated** a letter to my little brother, and he wrote down every word I said.

dictator *n.* A person who has complete control over a country; a person who is obeyed without question.
Hitler ruled Germany as a **dictator** from 1933 to 1945.

Ask your partner to dictate a sentence while you write it down.

exasperate
eg zas´ pər āt

v. To make angry; to annoy.
My brother **exasperates** my parents because he uses his phone so much.

exasperating *adj.* Very annoying.
Waiting in long lines to enter the stadium, before the game, can be quite **exasperating.**

notable
nōt´ ə bəl

adj. Deserving of attention; outstanding.
Michelle Obama was one of the most **notable** first ladies to ever occupy the White House.

overdue
ō vər dōō´

adj. 1. Coming later than expected or needed.
The bus from Boston is **overdue.**

2. Unpaid when owed.
My aunt never allows her bills to become **overdue.**

| **overthrow** | *v.* To end the rule of; to defeat, often by using force. |
| ō vər thrō′ | If we **overthrow** the king, who will take his place? |

overthrew *(past tense)*
The Polish people finally **overthrew** the Communist government that had been in power for more than forty years.

n. The action of overthrowing.
Countries sometimes attempt an **overthrow** of their ruler.

| **penetrate** | *v.* 1. To pierce. |
| pen′ ə trāt | Luckily, the piece of glass Irma stepped on did not **penetrate** her foot. |

2. To pass into or through.
Very little light **penetrated** the dense forest.

Discuss with your partner what to do if a rusty nail penetrates your skin.

| **portrait** | *n.* A drawing, painting, or photograph of a person, especially the face. |
| pôr′ trit | The famous **portrait** known as the *Mona Lisa* is in the Louvre, in Paris. |

| **rebel** | *n.* A person who refuses to obey orders or the law. |
| reb′ əl | If the **rebels** continue to gain popular support, they will be a serious threat to the government. |

v. (ri bel′) To refuse to accept control by others.
The small children **rebelled** when their parents told them to go to bed.

rebellious *adj.* (ri bel′ yəs) Fighting against another's control; disobedient.
Grounding is a punishment parents often use for **rebellious** children.

rebellion *n.* (ri bel′ yən) Open opposition to another's control.
The idea of year-round school made some students think of **rebellion.**

Tell your partner what school rule might make you want to rebel.

| **restrict** | *v.* To keep within certain limits. |
| rē strikt′ | We **restrict** this pathway to people riding bicycles. |

restriction *n.* A limit.
Our school has some **restrictions** about what students may wear.

Chat with your partner about why your school should or should not restrict classroom visitors.

| **seldom** | *adv.* Not often; rarely. |
| sel′ dəm | Because the sun's rays are so strong, we **seldom** spend the whole day at the beach. |

| **stimulate** | *v.* To make more active. |
| stim´ yōō lāt | The aroma of black bean soup from the kitchen **stimulated** my appetite for lunch. |

Talk with your partner about what could stimulate a dog to wake up from a nap.

| **tempest** | *n.* A violent windstorm usually with snow, rain, or hail. |
| tem´ pəst | A **tempest** at sea is a sailor's greatest fear. |

tempestuous *adj.* Stormy, wild.
After a **tempestuous** argument, the two friends agreed to disagree and ended the discussion.

| **upbringing** | *n.* The care and training a child gets while growing up. |
| up´ briŋ iŋ | My parents work very hard to give my brothers and me a wonderful **upbringing.** |

12A Using Words in Context

Read the following sentences. If the word in bold is used correctly, write C on the line. If the word is used incorrectly, write I on the line.

1. (a) The teacher **dictated** that no one could work together on the test. ____
   (b) One person should not **dictate** what happens to the whole group. ____
   (c) She **dictated** her speech to her secretary. ____
   (d) The park is **dictated** to everyone who enjoys it. ____

2. (a) A **rebellion** of yellow flowers covered the hillside. ____
   (b) My older sister has always been the **rebel** in our family. ____
   (c) It would cost **rebellions** of dollars to fix the broken windows. ____
   (d) Reading the long list of rules made us feel **rebellious.** ____

3. (a) The **tempest** at sea made boats race toward the harbor. ____
   (b) The feud became more **tempestuous** when neither person would apologize. ____
   (c) I closed the door softly because of the **tempest** sleeping in the bed. ____
   (d) The **tempest** moment came just before the end of the race. ____

4. (a) Active community members **dedicate** their lives to improving their neighborhoods. _____
   (b) The author **dedicated** her first novel to her family. _____
   (c) Ten dollars was **dedicated** from my purse. _____
   (d) The only **dedication** I took was a cough drop. _____

5. (a) I **restricted** my remarks to safe topics like the weather. _____
   (b) The trails are **restricted** to foot travel, which means no vehicles are allowed. _____
   (c) The **restrictions** tasted like lemon and mint. _____
   (d) I **restrict** myself to one hour of TV a day. _____

6. (a) Jorge **seldom** thinks of the house he grew up in. _____
   (b) Dad's favorite **seldom** is making sure we get to school safely. _____
   (c) Anya had a short **seldom** published in the school paper. _____
   (d) Since Kaysha moved to Seattle, I **seldom** hear from her. _____

7. (a) The **portrait** was done with watercolors and ink. _____
   (b) George Washington grew up in a **portrait** on a farm. _____
   (c) You have to show your **portrait** before boarding the school bus. _____
   (d) The two **portraits** show Frederick Douglass with and without a beard. _____

convalesce
dedicate
dictate
exasperate
notable
overdue
overthrow
penetrate
portrait
rebel
restrict
seldom
stimulate
tempest
upbringing

8. (a) The soldiers won a **notable** victory at Gettysburg. _____
   (b) We took a few **notables** with us in case we got hungry. _____
   (c) I made a **notable** in my diary that today was the first day of spring. _____
   (d) The score wasn't **notable** until the last seconds of the game. _____

9. (a) A person's **upbringing** should include the freedom to explore. _____
   (b) The **upbringing** of my birthday isn't necessary. _____
   (c) Maya's positive **upbringing** explains how kind she is to everyone. _____
   (d) We assembled the **upbringing** and set it in the corner. _____

10. (a) You pay a fine for library books that are **overdue.** _____
    (b) The plane is **overdue** because of strong winds. _____
    (c) I've learned to **overdue** the names of my friends. _____
    (d) I was able to **overdue** the others and won the race comfortably. _____

Making Connections

Circle the letter next to each correct answer. There may be more than one correct answer.

1. Which word or words go with *get better?*
   (a) dedicate   (b) revive   (c) restrict   (d) convalesce

2. Which word or words go with *believe something strongly?*
   (a) overdue   (b) confident   (c) exasperate   (d) notable

3. Which word or words go with *annoy?*
   (a) frustrate   (b) stimulate   (c) exasperate   (d) liberate

4. Which word or words go with *defeat?*
   (a) overthrow   (b) utilize   (c) restrict   (d) penetrate

5. Which word or words go with *enter into?*
   (a) penetrate   (b) bore   (c) exasperate   (d) pierce

6. Which word or words go with *more active?*
   (a) penetrate   (b) stimulate   (c) convalesce   (d) dictate

7. Which word or words go with *famous?*
   (a) notable   (b) exasperating   (c) tempestuous   (d) celebrated

8. Which word or words go with *lack of respect?*
   (a) hearty   (b) melancholy   (c) modest   (d) rebellious

9. Which word or words go with *how often?*
   (a) reassuringly   (b) seldom   (c) occasionally   (d) frequently

10. Which word or words go with *put a stop to?*
    (a) ban   (b) dedicate   (c) terminate   (d) restrict

12c Determining Meanings

Circle the letter next to each answer choice that correctly completes the sentence. There may be more than one correct answer.

1. She **dictated**
   (a) where and how people should live.
   (b) two sticks together to make a fire.
   (c) the dishes after midnight.
   (d) what time we should get up tomorrow.

2. **Tempestuous**
   (a) times are when we most need calm leadership.
   (b) weather kept the kids indoors.
   (c) emotions could be seen in the audience at the graduation.
   (d) creatures three stories high once roamed Earth.

3. An **overdue**
   (a) bill needs to be paid promptly.
   (b) book must be returned to the library.
   (c) remark can sometimes hurt a person's feelings.
   (d) train will be late coming into the station.

4. The **overthrown**
   (a) governor has not yet said anything to the press.
   (b) leader of the country was actually happy to not be in charge any longer.
   (c) ice is kept in a separate container.
   (d) wind turned the boat upside down and almost sank it.

5. I was **exasperated**
   (a) when I wasn't allowed into the concert.
   (b) for not being truthful when I was asked a question.
   (c) in an ambulance to the hospital emergency room.
   (d) to see my name had been left off the list.

6. The **dedication**
   (a) was to her parents and sisters.
   (b) was built in 1849 and is still standing.
   (c) at the cemetery entrance honored the lives of all those buried there.
   (d) of the new school took an hour, and then we went home.

convalesce
dedicate
dictate
exasperate
notable
overdue
overthrow
penetrate
portrait
rebel
restrict
seldom
stimulate
tempest
upbringing

7. Something **stimulated**
   (a) my appetite, and I suddenly felt hungry.
   (b) another painting for the wall.
   (c) on the chair in the corner of the room.
   (d) my curiosity, so I had to ask him why.

8. The artist's **portrait**
   (a) gurgled and growled hungrily.
   (b) is in the back of the museum.
   (c) drank a full gallon of milk.
   (d) is of a woman holding flowers.

12D Completing Sentences

Complete the sentences to demonstrate your knowledge of the words in bold.

1. If you **dedicate** your weekends to something, that means you

   _____.

2. One thing I find **exasperating** is

   _____.

3. A **portrait** of me would be of

   _____.

4. A good **upbringing** means having

   _____.

5. You need to **convalesce** if

   _____.

6. If a friendship is **tempestuous,** that means it is

   _____.

7. Something that **stimulates** my mind is

   _____.

8. The name of one **notable** person I know of is

   _____.

9. Something I **seldom** do is

_____.

10. To **penetrate** a piece of paper, you could

_____.

Vocabulary in Context

Read the passage.

A Child of the Revolution

Frida Kahlo was born in Coyoacan, just outside Mexico City, in 1907. Her parents probably thought her life would develop much as the lives of other girls of that time. The Mexican **dictator** Porfirio Diaz had been governing for almost thirty years. Under his rule women were **restricted** from taking any part in public life. Furthermore, Frida's parents gave her and her three sisters a strict Catholic **upbringing.** The girls were expected to be obedient daughters and to become good Catholic wives and mothers.

But in 1910, when Frida was three years old, everything changed in Mexico. The people **overthrew** Diaz and established a much more open government. The new government speedily set about making many changes that were long **overdue.** Education and health care became more widely available. More significantly for Frida Kahlo's future, the new government set out to **stimulate** interest in the arts by supporting the work of Mexican artists.

Her three sisters were largely unaffected by these changes. But Frida, who was the **rebellious** one, took part in them. She seemed to enjoy shocking people. One of the ways she did this was to go about wearing men's clothes. She was a firm supporter of the 1910 revolution; as an adult she claimed to have been born that year so that she could call herself "a child of the revolution." Her Mexican mother and German father must have despaired of her at times. They couldn't have known that their lively daughter would grow up to become one of Latin America's most **notable** painters.

Frida Kahlo had a difficult childhood. At the age of six she contracted polio. That left her with a weakened right leg. Then, in her late teens, she

convalesce
dedicate
dictate
exasperate
notable
overdue
overthrow
penetrate
portrait
rebel
restrict
seldom
stimulate
tempest
upbringing

suffered terrible injuries when she was thrown from a bus onto a metal spike. The spike **penetrated** her side, almost killing her.

While she **convalesced,** she began to paint. This was a way of taking her mind off the severe pain, from which she was **seldom** free for the rest of her life. Many of her paintings are self-**portraits;** in them she often included the parrots, monkeys, and other pets whose company gave her so much pleasure. Despite their bold, bright colors, however, the paintings clearly express the pain that lies behind them. Kahlo's art was her way of inviting the viewer to share her suffering.

She first met her future husband, the painter Diego Rivera, in 1922, when she was fifteen. They married seven years later. He was twice her age and already a world-famous artist. The marriage was a **tempestuous** one with many separations, a divorce, and later a remarriage. They both had strong personalities and each found the other **exasperating** to live with. Nevertheless, their love was strong and deep; Rivera appears frequently in her paintings.

Toward the end of her life, they lived together in the house where she was born, Casa Azul (the Blue House). After Kahlo's death in 1954, Rivera gave it to the people of Mexico. Now, known as the Frida Kahlo Museum, it is **dedicated** to her life and work. The fame of both artists has grown over the years. In 2015, the Detroit Institute of Arts brought together over seventy of their paintings and murals. The artwork on display showed clearly how much they had influenced each other's work.

▶ **Answer each of the following questions with a sentence. If a question does not contain a vocabulary word from the lesson's word list, use one in your answer. Use each word only once.**

1. What detail in the passage suggests that Porfirio Diaz was accustomed to being obeyed without question?

_____

_____

2. How did the Mexican people show their dissatisfaction with Porfirio Diaz?

_____

_____

3. How do you know that Kahlo's parents were not interested in experimenting with different ways of raising children?

_____

_____

4. Why would Mexican artists have welcomed the 1910 revolution?

_____

_____

5. Why do you think Kahlo's parents might sometimes have been **exasperated** with Frida?

_____

_____

6. What is the meaning of **overdue** as it is used in the passage?

_____

_____

7. In what way did Kahlo **rebel** against what was considered normal behavior?

_____

_____

8. How do you think Kahlo's weakened right leg affected her life?

_____

_____

9. Why did Kahlo probably lose a lot of blood in her accident?

_____

_____

10. What helped Kahlo **convalesce** after her accident?

_____

_____

11. What is the meaning of **dedicated** as it is used in the passage?

_____

_____

convalesce
dedicate
dictate
exasperate
notable
overdue
overthrow
penetrate
portrait
rebel
restrict
seldom
stimulate
tempest
upbringing

12. How does the passage make clear that Kahlo never recovered completely from the accident?

_____

_____

13. Why would it be incorrect to describe Rivera and Kahlo as a compatible couple?

_____

_____

14. What did Frida Kahlo paint?

_____

_____

15. Why are both Diego Rivera and Frida Kahlo honored in the world of art?

_____

_____

Fun & Fascinating FACTS

- **Dictate** is formed from the Latin verb *dicere,* which means "to say" or "to speak." Other words formed from this root include *diction,* "a person's manner or way of speaking," and *contradict,* "to say the opposite of."

- Three nouns are formed from the verb **stimulate.** *Stimulation* is the act of stimulating. (The aroma of freshly baked bread was the only *stimulation* we needed to enter the bakery.) A *stimulant* is a substance that increases bodily activity. (The caffeine in coffee and cola drinks is a *stimulant*.) A *stimulus* is anything that increases activity of any kind. (The reward of $50 was a *stimulus* to the children who were looking for the lost dog.)

restrict

verb 1. To limit someone's actions or movements.

2. To keep within certain limits.

Word Family
restricted (adjective)
restriction (noun)

Context Clues

These sentences give clues to the meaning of **restrict.**

> The use of smartphones or computers may be **restricted** during class, unless they are used for schoolwork.

> Because of Sofia's allergy, she had to **restrict** the amount of milk in her diet.

Discussion & Writing Prompt

*Paloma's parents put **restrictions** on TV time. As long as her homework is complete, she may watch TV between 7 p.m. and 9 p.m.*

After reading these sentences, what do you think **restriction** means? Write the definition and then use **restriction** in a sentence of your own.

2 min.	3 min.
1. Turn and talk to your partner or group.	2. Write 2–4 sentences.
Use this space to take notes or draw your ideas.	Be ready to share what you have written.

Review

Crossword Puzzle   Solve the crossword puzzle by studying the clues and filling in the answer boxes. The number after a clue is the lesson the word is from.

Clues Across

1. Not often **(12)**
4. A tied ball game goes into _____ innings
7. To chase after **(10)**
9. To walk in a relaxed, unhurried manner **(11)**
10. To copy closely **(9)**
11. To prepare; to make ready for a shock **(11)**
14. Opposite of *under*
15. To name or address as an honor **(12)**
17. To stop for a while before going on **(9)**
19. The state of being enslaved **(10)**
21. To give to a fund or cause **(10)**
22. A building where aircraft are kept **(11)**
23. It covers the floor
24. One who watches an activity **(9)**

Clues Down

2. To keep away from **(10)**
3. Tightly packed; crowded close together **(9)**
5. A violent storm **(12)**
6. To go to a higher level **(9)**
7. To go on after stopping for a while **(11)**
8. To fly high in the sky **(9)**
12. Opposite of *subtract*
13. To keep within certain limits **(12)**
14. Past the time set for arrival **(12)**
15. To give orders **(12)**
16. To get in touch with **(11)**
18. Planet known for its rings
20. Opposite of *sad*

Study the definitions of the words. Then do the exercises that follow.

accommodate
ə käm´ ə dat

v. 1. To have or to find room for.
This bus, which **accommodates** thirty adults, will drive to the historic buildings in the center of the city.

2. To do a favor for.
Tell me what you want, and I will try to **accommodate** you.

· ·

Ask your partner to tell you a favor you could do to accommodate him or her.

aggressive
ə gres´ iv

adj. 1. Ready to attack or start fights; acting in a hostile way.
Many animals become **aggressive** when their young are threatened.

2. Bold and active.
Serena Williams, the American tennis star, plays a talented and **aggressive** game.

· ·

Describe for your partner how an aggressive football player might act.

bask
bask

v. 1. To relax where it is pleasantly warm.
At lunch break, several students **basked** in the sunshine flooding the front steps.

2. To enjoy a warm or pleasant feeling.
The twins **basked** in the praise heaped on them by their parents.

carcass
kar´ kəs

n. The dead body of an animal.
We called the city to request that the raccoon **carcass** on our street be removed.

conceal
kən sēl´

v. To keep something or someone from being seen or known; to hide.
Playing hide-and-seek with my younger cousins, I **concealed** myself behind the kitchen door.

· ·

Conceal a pencil behind your back, and have your partner guess which hand it is in.

flail
flāl

v. To strike out or swing wildly; to thrash about.
Matt's arms **flailed** desperately after he jumped in the pool.

gorge
gôrj

n. A narrow passage between steep cliffs.
We crossed the **gorge** on a swaying rope bridge.

v. To stuff with food; to eat greedily.
The children **gorged** themselves on watermelon at the family picnic.

morsel
môr´ səl

n. A small amount, especially of something good to eat; a tidbit.
For appetizers we served stuffed mushrooms and other tasty **morsels.**

protrude
prō trōōd´

v. To stick out; to project.
Watch out for the stone ledge that **protrudes** from the wall.

. . . .

Chat with your partner about items that are so large they would protrude from your backpack, such as a baseball bat.

ripple
rip´ əl

v. To form small waves.
The breeze **rippled** the surface of the lake.

n. A movement like a small wave.
Raindrops made **ripples** in the pond.

. . . .

Talk to your partner about what the ripples might look like if you threw rocks into a pond or large puddle.

slither
slith´ ər

v. To move with a sliding, side-to-side motion of the body.
A snake **slithered** through the grass.

sluggish
slug´ ish

adj. 1. Lacking energy; not active.
The heat made me **sluggish.**

2. Slow moving.
In the dry season, the river becomes little more than a **sluggish** stream.

snout
snout

n. The nose or jaws that stick out in front of certain animals' heads.
The **snout** of a crocodile is full of long, sharp teeth.

taper
tā′ pər

v. 1. To make or become less wide or less thick at one end.
The little dog's tail **tapers** to a point.

2. To lessen gradually. (Usually used with *off*.)
When a loud knock was heard at the door, the professor's voice **tapered** off until she fell silent.

n. A thin candle.
The only light in the room came from a flickering **taper.**

Make a funny noise with your voice for your partner, and then taper off until you are silent.

visible
viz′ ə bəl

adj. Able to be seen; exposed to view; not hidden.
On a clear day Mount Shasta is **visible** from fifty miles away.

visibility *n.* 1. The condition of being easily seen.
An orange vest increases a cyclist's **visibility** on the road.

2. The distance within which things can be seen.
Visibility is poor this morning because of the fog.

Hold a small item behind your back, and then make it visible to your partner.

Finding Meanings

Choose two phrases to form a sentence that correctly uses a word from Word List 13. Then write the sentence.

1. (a) relax where it is pleasantly warm.
   (b) move by sliding from side to side.
   (c) To taper is to
   (d) To slither is to

_____

2. (a) An aggressive animal is one
   (b) A sluggish animal is one
   (c) that is a carnivore.
   (d) that is ready to fight.

_____

_____

3. (a) stuff oneself with food.   (c) To gorge is to
   (b) strike out wildly.   (d) To taper is to

_____

_____

4. (a) a small wave.   (c) A carcass is
   (b) a tasty bit of food.   (d) A ripple is

_____

_____

5. (a) To flail is to   (c) hold out one's arms.
   (b) To bask is to   (d) enjoy a pleasant feeling.

_____

_____

6. (a) within sight.   (c) lacking energy.
   (b) To be visible is to be (d) To be concealed is to be

_____

_____

7. (a) keep out of sight.   (c) strike out wildly.
   (b) To protrude is to   (d) To flail is to

_____

_____

8. (a) an animal's slow movement. (c) A morsel is
   (b) an animal's projecting nose. (d) A snout is

_____

_____

9. (a) speak favorably of that person. (c) hide that person.
   (b) To conceal someone is to   (d) To accommodate someone is to

_____

_____

10. (a) the body of a dead animal. (c) A carcass is
    (b) a narrow passage.   (d) A morsel is

_____

_____

13B Just the Right Word

Replace each phrase in bold with a single word (or form of the word) from the word list.

1. The company received an avalanche of mail the first day, but the orders soon **began to arrive in smaller and smaller numbers.**

2. A leaf dropped onto the pond and **made small waves on** the surface.

3. The **narrow passage with cliffs on either side** is two hundred feet deep.

4. Will you be able to **find room for** all five of us in your car?

5. When a **small piece of something good to eat** fell to the floor, we let our dog eat it.

6. Customers who cannot pay their bills are pursued by the company in a very **active and forceful** manner.

7. The Inuit hunters carried the **dead body of the animal** back to their village.

8. The twins **wildly swung** their arms and legs as their parents tried to dress them in snowsuits.

9. I am usually **very slow moving** on cold mornings.

10. Watch out! There are several rusty nails **sticking out** from that board lying on the ground in front of you.

| accommodate |
| aggressive |
| bask |
| carcass |
| conceal |
| flail |
| gorge |
| morsel |
| protrude |
| ripple |
| slither |
| sluggish |
| snout |
| taper |
| visible |

13C Applying Meanings

Circle the letter or letters next to each correct answer. There may be more than one correct answer.

1. Which of the following would decrease **visibility?**
   (a) fog
   (b) a telescope
   (c) a blizzard
   (d) darkness

2. Which of the following is an **aggressive** remark?
   (a) "Get out of my way!"
   (b) "I'm sorry."
   (c) "Forget it!"
   (d) "Would you please repeat that?"

3. Which of the following might make a person **sluggish?**
   (a) a heavy meal
   (b) bracing air
   (c) lying in the sun
   (d) a stimulant

4. Which of the following animals **slither?**
   (a) snakes
   (b) lizards
   (c) frogs
   (d) kangaroos

5. Which of the following can **taper?**
   (a) a twelve-inch ruler
   (b) the blade of a dinner knife
   (c) a candle
   (d) the toe of a shoe

6. Which of the following **protrudes** from the head?
   (a) the neck
   (b) the nose
   (c) the ears
   (d) the brain

7. In which of the following places might one **bask?**
   (a) on the beach
   (b) beside the pool
   (c) near a campfire
   (d) on a tropical island

8. Which of the following might **accommodate** your neighbors?
   (a) lending them your toys
   (b) inviting them to celebrate
   (c) denouncing them to your friends
   (d) watching their dog while they're away

13D Word Study: Synonyms

Each group of words contains two, three, or four synonyms. Circle any words that are NOT synonyms.

1. aggressive   visible   hostile   friendly

2. taper   conceal   hide   obscure

3. exasperate   annoy   infuriate   protrude

4. anxious   worried   concerned   nervous

5. exultant   joyful   sluggish   methodical

6. absurd   nonchalant   silly   ridiculous

7. heroic   brave   fearless   bold

8. interest   fascinate   donate   attract

9. feeble   evasive   puny   burly

10. yearn   loathe   dislike   hate

accommodate
aggressive
bask
carcass
conceal
flail
gorge
morsel
protrude
ripple
slither
sluggish
snout
taper
visible

Beware the Silent Crocodile

Crocodiles are the largest and most ferocious of all reptiles. They live in swampy areas, close to the banks of tropical rivers or lakes. They have been around since the age of the dinosaurs. Back then they reached lengths of thirty feet or more. The crocodile of today, however, is much smaller than its ancient ancestors. It seldom grows longer than fifteen feet from its head to the tip of its long, **tapering** tail.

Crocodiles in the wild are almost unknown in North America. A few can be found in the remaining tidal marshes of the Everglades and the Florida Keys. There they might be mistaken for alligators, their close relatives. Crocodiles and alligators resemble each other in many ways. There are clear differences between them, however. The crocodile is the more **aggressive** of the two. It also has a longer and narrower **snout,** and the fourth tooth on each side of its jaw **protrudes.** That tooth remains in view even when its mouth is closed.

A crocodile in the water lies almost entirely **concealed** below the surface; only its eyes and nostrils are **visible.** It can stay like this for hours, its eyes fixed on the water's edge, waiting for a thirsty animal to come to drink. When this happens, the crocodile is careful not to scare away its prey. It disappears beneath the surface, swimming slowly toward the unsuspecting animal; it makes not even the slightest **ripple.**

If the thirsty animal is lucky, it senses the danger in time and escapes. If the crocodile is lucky, it seizes the animal in its jaws, knocks it off balance by **flailing** its powerful tail, and drags it into the water. There the creature drowns. The crocodile then finds a place where it can **gorge** on the dead animal without being disturbed. When it has eaten its fill, it will hide the remains of the **carcass.** Then it will return to feed on it later.

When not hunting for food, the crocodile spends much of its time on land. Its belly almost touches the ground as it **slithers** from the water and finds a comfortable spot to **bask** in the sun. Like other reptiles, the crocodile is a cold-blooded animal; therefore, its temperature changes with its surroundings. To escape the extreme heat of midday, it burrows into the soft ground with its sharp claws until it has made a hole large enough to **accommodate** itself. In the cool of the evening, its temperature drops and its movements become **sluggish.**

There are several different kinds of crocodile. The best known is the Nile crocodile of Africa, which has an unusual companion called the crocodile bird. This daring little creature feeds by hopping inside the crocodile's mouth and picking **morsels** of meat from its teeth. The crocodile shows its gratitude for having its teeth cleaned in this way by not eating the bird.

▶ **Answer each of the following questions with a sentence. If a question does not contain a vocabulary word from the lesson's word list, use one in your answer. Use each word only once.**

1. Why is it unwise to get too close to a crocodile?

_____

_____

2. How does the shape of a crocodile's head differ from that of an alligator?

_____

_____

3. What do crocodiles and snakes have in common?

_____

_____

4. What is the shape of a crocodile's tail?

_____

_____

5. Why do crocodiles hide the **carcasses** of animals they have killed?

_____

_____

6. When are crocodiles likely to be slow in their movements?

_____

_____

7. What is the meaning of **bask** as it is used in the passage?

_____

_____

8. What parts of a crocodile are **visible** when it is waiting for prey?

_____

_____

| accommodate |
| aggressive |
| bask |
| carcass |
| conceal |
| flail |
| gorge |
| morsel |
| protrude |
| ripple |
| slither |
| sluggish |
| snout |
| taper |
| visible |

9. How does a crocodile use its tail to overcome its prey?

_____

_____

10. What is the meaning of **accommodate** as it is used in the passage?

_____

_____

11. What does the crocodile do after it drowns its prey?

_____

_____

12. Why is the prey of a crocodile unlikely to see it approaching in the water?

_____

_____

13. Why do you think the crocodile's eyes and nostrils **protrude** above the surface when it is in the water?

_____

_____

14. What do crocodile birds eat?

_____

_____

15. Why do crocodiles lie **concealed** in the water for long periods of time?

_____

_____

Fun & Fascinating **FACTS**

- A *slug* is like a snail but without the shell; it moves very slow. *Slug* comes from an old Scandinavian word *slugje*, which means "a heavy, slow person." The noun *sluggard*, "a lazy, slow-moving person" and the adjective **sluggish** are formed from this word.

- Don't confuse *tapir*, the name for a large piglike animal that lives in the forests of Central and South America, with **taper.** These two words sound the same but have different meanings and spellings.

visible

adjective Able to be seen; not hidden.

Word Family
invisible (adjective)
invisibility (noun)
visibility (noun)

Word Parts
The suffix *-able/-ible* means "able to."
Other words with this suffix are *flexible* and *responsible*. What are some other words with the suffix *-able/-ible*?

Discussion & Writing Prompt

If *in-* means "not" and *visible* means "able to be seen," what does **invisible** mean? Use this information to also define *incorrect* and *inactive*.

2 min.	3 min.
1. Turn and talk to your partner or group.	2. Write 2–4 sentences.
Use this space to take notes or draw your ideas.	Be ready to share what you have written.

Word List

Study the definitions of the words. Then do the exercises that follow.

access
ak´ ses

n. 1. Freedom or permission to enter.
The students want **access** to the gym this summer.

2. A way of approach or entry.
The only **access** to the harbor is this channel.

accessible *adj.* Able to be used or entered.
Franklin's Restaurant is **accessible** to people in wheelchairs.

Discuss with your partner how libraries make books accessible to everyone.

associate
ə sō´ shē āt

v. 1. To bring together in the mind.
Many people **associate** Florida with oranges.

2. To come or be together as friends or companions.
Because of her love of racehorses, Anne often **associated** with others who shared that love—jockeys and trainers.

n. (ə sō´ shē ət) A person with whom one is connected in some way, as in business.
My father discussed a project with his **associate** at work.

boisterous
bois´ tər əs

adj. Noisy and uncontrolled.
The Dixons' party became so **boisterous** that their neighbors complained.

brilliant
bril´ yənt

adj. 1. Very bright; sparkling.
My black leather shoes had a **brilliant** shine.

2. Very clever or smart.
My oldest sister is so **brilliant** she might finish high school in three years.

decade
dek´ ād

n. A ten-year period.
I have hope that the next **decade** will be better than the last.

Share with your partner what you hope you will be doing one decade from now.

delicate
del´i kət

adj. 1. Easily broken or damaged.
We always wash this **delicate** antique plate by hand.

2. Needing care and skill.
Convincing small children to share a toy can be a **delicate** task.

3. In poor health; weak.
Although Isabella Bird Bishop was a **delicate** child, as an adult, she traveled through many different parts of the world, sometimes by canoe and other times on horseback.

employ
em ploi´

v. 1. To hire and put to work for pay.
Carmen's gift shop **employs** four people.

2. To use.
The clown **employed** every trick he knew to make the children laugh.

Tell your partner what tools you employ when you work on math problems.

idle
ī´ dəl

adj. Doing nothing; not working.
The workers were **idle** while the power was shut off.

v. 1. To spend one's time doing nothing.
Last Sunday, while my brother **idled** for more than an hour in the house, I raked leaves in the yard.

2. To run (an engine) slowly.
Let the car **idle** for a few minutes so that the engine can warm up.

illuminate
il loo´ mə nāt

v. 1. To light up; to supply with light.
The full moon **illuminated** the path through the woods to our cabin.

2. To make clear or understandable.
The teacher's explanation **illuminated** the math problem for me.

Illuminate for your partner the meaning of the previous word in the word list.

provide
prō vīd´

v. 1. To give what is needed; to supply.
Two local companies **provided** the money to buy our school band uniforms.

2. To set forth as a condition.
Our agreement with the teacher **provides** for a party if we turn our work in on time all year.

Chat with your partner about what you think parents should provide for their children.

require rē kwīr´	*v.* To need or demand. Plants **require** light and water in order to grow. **requirement** *n.* Something that is necessary. A place to sleep and a simple meal were Johnny Appleseed's only **requirements.**

Discuss with your partner what things a dog requires to be safe.

taunt tônt	*v.* To make fun of in an insulting way; to jeer. Don't **taunt** someone just because that person appears different. *n.* An insulting remark. An umpire learns to ignore the **taunts** of the crowd and just get on with the job.

tolerant täl´ ər ənt	*adj.* Willing to let others have their own beliefs and ways, even if different from one's own. Traveling is both interesting and enjoyable if you are **tolerant** of customs that seem strange to you. **tolerate** *v.* To accept willingly and without complaining. You learn to **tolerate** a certain amount of noise when you live near an airport.

transform trans fôrm´	*v.* To change the form, looks, or nature of. A fresh coat of paint will **transform** this room. **transformation** *n.* A complete change. The **transformation** of the frog into a prince comes at the end of the story.

Tell your partner how you would plan the transformation of your bedroom if you could do whatever you wanted.

wilderness wil´ dər nəs	*n.* An area where there are few people living; an area still in its natural state. The Rocky Mountain states contain large areas of **wilderness.**

14A Using Words in Context

Read the following sentences. If the word in bold is used correctly, write C on the line. If the word is used incorrectly, write I on the line.

1. (a) Use as much paint as you need and throw the **access** away. ____
   (b) My sister has **access** to all the clothes in my closet, too. ____
   (c) The only **access** to the theater was through the stage door. ____
   (d) The top shelf was only **accessible** when using a stool. ____

2. (a) The glass ornaments are **delicate** and must be handled carefully. ____
   (b) Igasho's fear of cats was a **delicate** subject that we never talked about. ____
   (c) A person in **delicate** health is told to stay home during flu season. ____
   (d) Chocolate candy and other **delicates** were laid out on the counter. ____

3. (a) The **brilliants** were full of water. ____
   (b) It took a team of **brilliant** minds to crack the secret code. ____
   (c) A **brilliant** emerald ring sold for fifteen hundred dollars. ____
   (d) Using lots of **brilliant** will make your teeth shine. ____

4. (a) Some viruses become **tolerant** of drugs developed to fight them. ____
   (b) Living with siblings makes you **tolerant** of other people. ____
   (c) The weather had become more **tolerant** by the time May arrived. ____
   (d) My teacher **tolerated** my report a good grade. ____

5. (a) Within a few years, the invention of the airplane had **transformed** travel. ____
   (b) We were **transformed** that the restaurant was closed for the evening. ____
   (c) The man closed the door with a **transformation.** ____
   (d) The beautiful day was suddenly **transformed** into a stormy mess. ____

6. (a) The **illuminates** flickered and went out, leaving us in total darkness. ____
   (b) A beam of sunlight **illuminated** the tree. ____
   (c) What the teacher said **illuminated** something I hadn't understood before. ____
   (d) I became more and more **illuminated** as I turned out the lights. ____

access
associate
boisterous
brilliant
decade
delicate
employ
idle
illuminate
provide
require
taunt
tolerant
transform
wilderness

7. (a) The **idle** child was too lazy to get out of bed in the morning. ____
   (b) We didn't have one **idle** moment during the whole trip. ____
   (c) Allow the engine to **idle** for a minute before turning it off. ____
   (d) The magazine was full of pictures of Hollywood movie **idles**. ____

8. (a) Try not to **employ** the flowers before they're fully bloomed. ____
   (b) The tire factory **employs** over five thousand people. ____
   (c) Davonne **employed** a brilliant attack that won the video game. ____
   (d) We **employed** her to stay longer, but her mind was made up. ____

9. (a) Visitors to the park are **required** to keep dogs on leashes. ____
   (b) You are **required** to check your backpack at the gate. ____
   (c) Give me a hug before I **require** for the night. ____
   (d) There were many **requires** to be answered after I got back. ____

10. (a) Eight **associate** justices and one chief justice form the
        Supreme Court. ____
    (b) I **associate** Florida with the beach. ____
    (c) We **associated** with all kinds of people during our field trip. ____
    (d) Tomiko grew more and more **associated** as the days passed. ____

14B Making Connections

Circle the letter next to each correct answer. There may be more than one correct answer.

1. Which word or words go with *weak?*
   (a) puny   (b) brilliant   (c) feeble   (d) delicate

2. Which word or words go with *not busy?*
   (a) idle   (b) boisterous   (c) sluggish   (d) tolerant

3. Which word or words go with *make fun of?*
   (a) humiliate   (b) transform   (c) taunt   (d) dedicate

4. Which word or words go with *change?*
   (a) transform   (b) provide   (c) employ   (d) associate

5. Which word or words go with *forest?*
   (a) suspect   (b) wilderness   (c) bondage   (d) taunt

6. Which word or words go with *smart?*
   (a) shrewd   (b) delicate   (c) boisterous   (d) brilliant

7. Which word or words go with *easygoing?*
   (a) patient   (b) tolerant   (c) rebellious   (d) tempestuous

8. Which word or words go with *give?*
   (a) provide   (b) employ   (c) donate   (d) transform

9. Which word or words go with *time?*
   (a) duration   (b) century   (c) decade   (d) requirement

10. Which word or words go with *uncontrolled?*
   (a) boisterous   (b) delicate   (c) spacious   (d) tolerant

access
associate
boisterous
brilliant
decade
delicate
employ
idle
illuminate
provide
require
taunt
tolerant
transform
wilderness

Circle the letter next to each answer choice that correctly completes the sentence. There may be more than one correct answer.

1. We **associated**
   (a) the kangaroos with Australia.
   (b) with all kinds of people.
   (c) crossing your fingers with good luck.
   (d) the ball back and forth before the game.

2. The **illumination**
   (a) of the pictures on the wall make them show up better at night.
   (b) of nostalgic thoughts occupy my mind.
   (c) in the dirt was cleaned off the sidewalk.
   (d) suddenly hit me—I knew the answer to the math problem.

3. You **provided**
   (a) whatever was needed to get the project started.
   (b) for those who depended on you.
   (c) that you can be trusted.
   (d) the cake into eight pieces.

4. The **requirement**
   (a) for attending the lunch was to choose between pizza or a veggie burger.
   (b) at recess was extremely tall and skinny.
   (c) to dance was full of sunshine and meadows.
   (d) before riding the Ferris wheel was to read the warning.

5. The **taunting**
   (a) kept us dry when it started to rain.
   (b) on the shirt came off in the wash.
   (c) of the crowd didn't bother him at all.
   (d) rang in my ears for the rest of the day.

6. **Employment**
   (a) is promised to the first twenty people who apply.
   (b) of all the wood will make the biggest bonfire.
   (c) on the sunflower seeds, water, and soil.
   (d) number 507 is on the fifth floor.

7. A **boisterous**

    (a) look from my mom told me I was in trouble.

    (b) child should be told to calm down.

    (c) party can be annoying to the neighbors.

    (d) relaxation spread over me.

8. Leon **accessed**

    (a) the house through the back door.

    (b) if he could take the test tomorrow.

    (c) into the tissue.

    (d) the mine by traveling down the shaft.

14D Completing Sentences

Complete the sentences to demonstrate your knowledge of the words in bold.

1. If you are in **delicate** health, that means you

    _____.

2. A **brilliant** scientist is one who

    _____.

3. Something I often **tolerate** is

    _____.

4. An example of a **taunt** might be

    _____.

5. One **requirement** for college is

    _____.

6. If someone is an **associate,** he or she is

    _____.

7. Something I **provided** today was

    _____.

8. In the **wilderness,** you will find

    _____.

access
associate
boisterous
brilliant
decade
delicate
employ
idle
illuminate
provide
require
taunt
tolerant
transform
wilderness

9. To **access** my bedroom, I need to

_____ .

10. I like to spend my **idle** time by

_____ .

Vocabulary in Context
Read the passage.

The Wizard of Menlo Park

Like other cities and towns in the late 1800s, New York City was a gloomy place at night. Streets were lit by flickering gas lights, if they were lit at all. Oil lamps or candles were all that people had to **illuminate** their homes. Thomas Edison had a better idea. In 1881, he built the world's first electric power station in Manhattan. He helped change New York into the **brilliantly** lit city we know today.

Edison was born in Ohio in 1847. When he was a small child, his family moved to Port Huron, Michigan. An attack of scarlet fever left him in **delicate** health. This worried his parents; they did not allow him to join in the **boisterous** games played at his school. The other children were not very **tolerant** of someone who stood apart from the rest, and young Edison had to suffer their **taunts.** His mother, who was a teacher, decided to take him out of school. She taught him at home, where he learned quickly. He asked many questions and liked to experiment on his own to find answers.

At that time, much of Michigan was **wilderness.** But the railroad was **transforming** America by making even the most remote places **accessible** to the rest of the country. When the railroad came to Port Huron, it **provided** Edison with his first job. At the age of twelve, he was given permission to sell newspapers and candy on the train that ran between his hometown and Detroit. He even printed his own newspaper, which he sold for three cents a copy.

At sixteen, he started working full time on the railroad. For the next four years, he was **employed** as a telegraph operator in different towns. However, there were large portions of the day when he had nothing to do, and Thomas Edison hated to be **idle.** In addition, he **required** only five or six hours of sleep a night. So it was during this time that he began working on inventions along with his experiments.

At twenty-one, he invented an electrical vote counter, for which he was given a patent. This meant that the government identified him as the person who thought up the idea and protected it so that it could not be made or sold by others without his permission. When he was thirty, Edison established a research center at Menlo Park, New Jersey. There he and his **associates** ran what was really an inventions factory.

Over the next five **decades,** Edison was granted over a thousand patents by the United States government. Perhaps his most famous invention was the electric light bulb. Other inventions included the record player (which he called a phonograph) and the movie camera. These things seemed like magic to people; it isn't surprising that he became known as the "Wizard of Menlo Park." The once sickly child outlived most of his schoolmates—when he died in 1931, he was eighty-four years old.

▶ **Answer each of the following questions with a sentence. If a question does not contain a vocabulary word from the lesson's word list, use one in your answer. Use each word only once.**

1. How does the passage make clear that there were few towns in Michigan during Edison's youth?

_____

_____

2. In what way was the railroad important in Edison's early life?

_____

_____

3. With what invention do most people **associate** Edison?

_____

_____

4. What is the meaning of **illuminate** as it is used in the passage?

_____

_____

access
associate
boisterous
brilliant
decade
delicate
employ
idle
illuminate
provide
require
taunt
tolerant
transform
wilderness

5. Why might Edison have been reluctant to go to school?

_____

_____

6. What **boisterous** activities might Edison's schoolmates have engaged in?

_____

_____

7. What details in the passage show that Edison's mother would not **tolerate** the behavior of Edison's classmates?

_____

_____

8. What is the meaning of **delicate** as it is used in the passage?

_____

_____

9. Why did Edison have **access** to the train from Port Huron to Detroit?

_____

_____

10. As a young man, how did Edison **employ** a lot of his free time?

_____

_____

11. What is the meaning of **idle** as it is used in the passage?

_____

_____

12. How did Edison change New York City?

_____

_____

13. How would you describe Edison's mind?

_____

_____

14. What must one do to protect a new invention from being copied by others?

_____

_____

15. How long did Edison live?

_____

_____

Fun & Fascinating FACTS

- Several nouns are formed from the verb **employ.** An *employee* is a person who works for someone else and is paid for this. An *employer* is a person who gives work to others and pays them. *Employment* is the state of having work or the work itself.

- **Idle** and *idol* are homophones. An *idol* is something, such as a carved figure, that is worshiped as a god. It can also be a person, such as an author, who is admired.

- **Illuminate** comes from *lumen,* the Latin word for "light." Other English words that are formed from this root include *luminous,* which means "glowing with light," and *luminosity,* which refers to the amount of light given off from something—for example, from a star. (One of the stars with the greatest *luminosity* that we can see without a telescope, apart from our own sun, is Sirius, also known as the Dog Star.)

access

associate

boisterous

brilliant

decade

delicate

employ

idle

illuminate

provide

require

taunt

tolerant

transform

wilderness

transform

verb To completely change the form or look of something, usually in a good way.

Word Family
transformation (noun)
transformed (verb)

Word Parts
The prefix *trans-* means "across" or "change."
Another word with this prefix is *transport*. What are some other words with the prefix *trans-?*

Discussion & Writing Prompt

During the duckling's **transformation** *into an adult, the gray, fuzzy feathers on its head turned bright green.*

Based on this sentence, write the definition of **transformation** and then use it in a new sentence of your own.

`2 min.`	`3 min.`
1. Turn and talk to your partner or group.	2. Write 2–4 sentences.
Use this space to take notes or draw your ideas.	Be ready to share what you have written.

Study the definitions of the words. Then do the exercises that follow.

disaster
di zas´ tər

n. Something that causes great damage or harm.
Hurricane Katrina was the worst **disaster** to hit New Orleans in many years.

disastrous *adj.* Causing much damage or harm.
The **disastrous** floods in the Midwest left many people homeless.

flee
flē

v. To run away from danger or from something frightening.
I quickly decided to **flee** from the park when I heard a noise behind me.

fled *(past tense)*
We **fled** from the house when we awoke and smelled gas.

 Discuss with your partner some situations from which you might need to flee.

fracture
frak´ chər

n. A crack or break, as in metal or bone.
The plane was grounded because of a small **fracture** in the metal tail unit.

v. To crack or break.
Selena **fractured** her arm for the second time this summer when she fell from the swing.

immense
im mens´

adj. 1. Great in size or extent.
The Pacific Ocean is an **immense** body of water.

2. Great in degree.
To the **immense** relief of his parents, the lost child was soon found.

 Tell your partner which is more immense—a puddle or an ocean.

intense
in tens´

adj. 1. Very strong; very great.
The **intense** heat from the fire melted the plastic dishes.

2. Showing great depth of feeling.
The scene in the play where the enslaved people are liberated from bondage is so **intense** that the audience often weeps.

intensity *n.* Great strength or force.
The **intensity** of light from the sun is greatest at noon.

 Chat with your partner about how you could describe the intensity of the wind in a tornado.

| **investigate** | *v.* To look into closely; to study in great detail. |
| in ves´ tə gāt | The fire marshal will **investigate** the cause of the fire in the library. |

lurch	*v.* To move forward or to one side suddenly and unexpectedly.
lʊrch	The car **lurched** to the left to avoid a bird on the road.
	n. A jerking or swaying movement.
	The bus started with a **lurch,** throwing the standing passengers off balance.

major	*adj.* Great in size, number, or importance.
mā´ jər	Seas and oceans make up the **major** part of the earth's surface.
	n. 1. A military officer just above a captain in rank.
	A colonel is superior in rank to a **major.**
	2. The main subject a student is studying.
	My **major** in college will be Russian Language and Literature.
	v. To study as one's most important subject.
	My cousin Karen **majored** in chemistry and mathematics at Community College.

Tell your partner about a hobby that takes up a major part of your weekends.

minor	*adj.* 1. Small; unimportant.
mī´ nər	Steffi's knee injury was **minor,** so she finished the game.
	n. A person who is not yet an adult; a child.
	Minors may attend this movie if an adult goes with them.

Discuss with your partner a minor change you would like to make in the way your classroom is set up.

petrify	*v.* 1. To make rigid with terror; to terrify.
pe´ tri fī	The director said that he felt his horror movies had failed if they did not **petrify** audiences.
	2. To change into a stonelike substance.
	In Arizona's Painted Desert, we saw examples of wood that had **petrified** over millions of years.

predict	*v.* To say what will happen before it takes place.
prē dikt´	The highway safety office **predicts** heavy traffic on the roads this weekend.
	prediction *n.* Something that is predicted.
	The **prediction** of a blizzard kept people from traveling last night.

Share with your partner what you predict for your future.

prone	*adj.* 1. Likely to have or do.
prōn	All of us are more **prone** to colds in the winter than in the summer.
	2. Lying face downward.
	I had to lie in a **prone** position because my back was so sunburned.

Talk to your partner about whether you are prone to be calm or worried on a busy day.

sparse	*adj.* 1. Thinly grown or spread.
spärs	The grass on the ball field was **sparse,** so we reseeded it.
	2. Not crowded.
	The town meeting had a **sparse** turnout this year.

topple	*v.* 1. To fall or push over.
täp´ əl	The cat **toppled** the pile of books.
	2. To overthrow.
	The student demonstrations helped **topple** the government.

| **urban** | *adj.* Having to do with cities. |
| ʉr´ bən | Traffic in **urban** areas is a serious problem during rush hour. |

15A

Finding Meanings

Choose two phrases to form a sentence that correctly uses a word from Word List 15. Then write the sentence.

1. (a) is one that is small and scattered.
   (b) A sparse crowd
   (c) is one that is very cold.
   (d) An immense crowd

   _____

   _____

2. (a) To investigate someone is to
   (b) terrify that person.
   (c) To petrify someone is to
   (d) come to that person's aid.

   _____

   _____

3. (a) An intense pain is one that   (c) A minor pain is one that
   (b) lasts for a long time.   (d) is very great.

   _____

   _____

4. (a) A prone figure is one   (c) that stands alone.
   (b) that is lying facedown.   (d) A fleeing figure is one

   _____

   _____

5. (a) keep it from happening.   (c) look into it closely.
   (b) To predict an accident is to   (d) To investigate an accident is to

   _____

   _____

6. (a) a person who works in a mine.   (c) A minor is
   (b) a person who is not yet   (d) A major is
       an adult.

   _____

   _____

7. (a) To lurch is to   (c) lie in a facedown position.
   (b) To flee is to   (d) move to the side suddenly.

   _____

   _____

8. (a) A prediction is   (c) a reminder of a past event.
   (b) A disaster is   (d) a forecast of what will happen.

   _____

   _____

9. (a) a student's main subject.   (c) A fracture is
   (b) a small wavelike movement.   (d) A major is

   _____

   _____

10. (a) An immense area is one   (c) that is very large.
    (b) An urban area is one   (d) that has few people.

    _____

    _____

Just the Right Word

Replace each phrase in bold with a single word (or form of the word) from the word list.

1. We **ran away** when the dog behind the flimsy gate started barking.

2. Much of the eastern United States that was wilderness in the 1700s is now **made up of cities and towns.**

3. The fire was a **terrible event that caused great damage,** but, fortunately, no lives were lost.

4. The car's **sudden movement** to the right told my dad we had a flat tire.

5. The **crack or break** in my arm took several weeks to heal.

6. The wood is millions of years old and has slowly **turned into a stonelike substance.**

7. The crossing guard's **first and most important** concern is the safety of the children as they are walking to school.

8. The **great force** of the speaker's words brought silence to the large crowd gathered for the memorial service.

9. Premature babies are **very likely** to suffer from lung problems.

10. The Mexican people **ended the rule of** President Diaz in 1910.

disaster
flee
fracture
immense
intense
investigate
lurch
major
minor
petrify
predict
prone
sparse
topple
urban

15c Applying Meanings

Circle the letter or letters next to each correct answer. There may be more than one correct answer.

1. Which of the following would you expect to see in an **urban** area?
   - (a) farm animals
   - (b) dirt roads
   - (c) neon signs
   - (d) skyscrapers

2. Which of the following could be **disastrous?**
   - (a) an avalanche
   - (b) a blizzard
   - (c) an accomplishment
   - (d) a voyage

3. Which of the following might one **predict?**
   - (a) what happened last year
   - (b) a blizzard
   - (c) the result of an election
   - (d) the result of an experiment

4. Which of the following is a **minor** injury?
   - (a) a scratched finger
   - (b) a pulled muscle
   - (c) a severed finger
   - (d) a small bruise

5. Which of the following is a **fracture?**
   - (a) a broken leg
   - (b) a broken promise
   - (c) a broken heart
   - (d) a broken arm

6. Which of the following would be visible on a **prone** person?
   - (a) the stomach
   - (b) the nose
   - (c) the back
   - (d) the knees

7. Which of the following might one **investigate?**
   - (a) a decade
   - (b) an explosion
   - (c) a crime
   - (d) an accident

8. Which of the following can be **toppled?**
   - (a) a tower
   - (b) a government
   - (c) a stack of books
   - (d) a statue

Write the antonym of each of the words on the left in the space next to it. Choose from the words on the right, which are in a different order.

1. immense _____ shy

2. major _____ mild

3. brilliant _____ obedient

4. delicate _____ calm

5. idle _____ tiny

6. conceal _____ minor

7. seldom _____ sturdy

8. confident _____ dim

9. rebellious _____ thick

10. tempestuous _____ busy

11. intense _____ reveal

12. sparse _____ often

| disaster |
| flee |
| fracture |
| immense |
| intense |
| investigate |
| lurch |
| major |
| minor |
| petrify |
| predict |
| prone |
| sparse |
| topple |
| urban |

When the Earth Quakes

Those who have lived through an earthquake describe it as one of the worst experiences of their lives. When one strikes, often without warning, people are usually too **petrified** to move. The ground, which a few moments before seemed so solid, suddenly **lurches** beneath their feet. Pictures are shaken from the walls. If the earthquake is severe enough, the walls themselves may **topple.** Water and gas pipes burst, fires flare up, and lives may be lost.

The **intensity** of an earthquake is determined by a measure called the Richter scale. An earthquake measuring 4.0 is considered **minor,** causing little, if any, harm. One measuring 8.0 is more than one thousand times as powerful; it can do **immense** damage. Another measure of the destructive power of an earthquake is the number of lives lost. One of the greatest natural **disasters** in history was the earthquake that struck China in 1556. That earthquake killed almost a million people.

Earthquakes do the greatest damage in **urban** areas where people are heavily concentrated. Most of the deaths and injuries occur when people are inside collapsing buildings. The San Francisco earthquake of 1906 measured 8.3 and killed 450 people. In 1964, Alaska, which is more **sparsely** settled, also experienced an earthquake measuring 8.3; there were fewer than 200 deaths there.

Scientists who **investigate** the causes of earthquakes are called seismologists. They have learned a great deal about these frightening occurrences. We know that the earth's crust, or surface, is made of rock five to twenty miles thick. That crust is **fractured** in many places. The separate pieces, or plates, fit more or less together along the break lines, which are known as "faults." Heat from the earth's interior puts pressure on these plates, causing them to move. Sometimes they rub against each other edge to edge; at other times one plate may ride up over another. These kinds of movements cause earthquakes.

Areas that lie along faults in the earth's crust are especially **prone** to earthquakes. But quakes can occur anywhere in the world. San Francisco lies on the San Andreas Fault, where the Pacific and North American plates meet. It has had two **major** earthquakes in the last century. The

Pacific coast regions of Central and South America, where the Nazca and South American plates meet, have also suffered many earthquakes and will continue to do so.

Unfortunately, we still do not know enough about earthquakes to be able to **predict** accurately when one will occur. We do, however, make sure that today's buildings and bridges are strong enough to stand up to them. That is one reason why the 1989 San Francisco earthquake, which measured 6.9 on the Richter scale, took so few lives. But earthquakes are still to be feared. If you should have the misfortune to get caught in one, your first thought might be to **flee** to the nearest open space. Experts tell us, however, that if you are in a modern building, it is probably safer to stay inside. Look for shelter under a sturdy table or in a doorway.

▶ **Answer each of the following questions with a sentence. If a question does not contain a vocabulary word from the lesson's word list, use one in your answer. Use each word only once.**

1. What do seismologists do?

_____

_____

2. What do the instruments used by seismologists measure?

_____

_____

3. Why did scientists not know the 1989 San Francisco earthquake was coming?

_____

_____

4. What **urban** area is on the San Andreas Fault?

_____

_____

5. What is the meaning of **topple** as it is used in the passage?

_____

_____

disaster
flee
fracture
immense
intense
investigate
lurch
major
minor
petrify
predict
prone
sparse
topple
urban

6. What might cause people to fall during an earthquake?

_____

_____

7. What is the meaning of **minor** as it is used in the passage?

_____

_____

8. How might a person describe what it feels like to live through an earthquake?

_____

_____

9. What would be the result of an earthquake in a city with many flimsy buildings?

_____

_____

10. How serious would an earthquake measuring 7.8 on the Richter scale be?

_____

_____

11. In what kind of area is an earthquake likely to do the least damage?

_____

_____

12. Why do you think streets are often flooded after an earthquake?

_____

_____

13. What is the meaning of **prone** as it is used in the passage?

_____

_____

14. How great was the loss of life in China's 1556 earthquake?

_____

_____

15. During an earthquake, is it a good idea to **flee** to an open space? Why or why not?

_____

_____

disaster

flee

fracture

immense

intense

investigate

lurch

major

minor

petrify

predict

prone

sparse

topple

urban

Fun & Fascinating FACTS

- This is an *asterisk:* *. It looks like a star, and in fact the word comes from the Latin word for "star," which is *aster*. **Disaster** comes from the Latin prefix *dis-,* which means "against," and *aster*. But what does a disaster have to do with the stars? It was once believed (and still is, by some people) that the position of the stars had an effect on people's daily lives. If something bad (a *disaster*) happened to you, it was because the *stars* were *against* you.

Two other words formed from this same root are *astronomy,* the scientific study of planets and stars, and *astrology,* the belief that the stars have an effect on people's daily lives.

- **Flee** and *flea* are homophones. A flea is a small jumping insect. **Minor** and *miner* are also homophones. A miner is a person who works in a mine, digging for coal, gold, or other minerals.

- If you *break* a leg, you have a **fracture.** If you drop a cup, it will *break* into *fragments.* If you *break* down the number 1 into smaller parts, such as halves, you get *fractions.* Something easily *broken* is *fragile.* All four of these words come from the Latin *frangere* or *fractus,* which means "to break."

- The Latin prefix *pre-* means "before." A *premature* baby is one born *before* it is *mature* enough to leave the womb. Knowing this, and keeping in mind the explanation of *dictate* at the very end of Lesson 12, you should be able to understand how **predict** is formed.

investigate

verb To study; to find out information about something or someone.

Academic Context

You **investigate** many things in science, such as what causes the weather.

Word Family

investigation (noun)
investigative (adjective)
investigator (noun)

Discussion & Writing Prompt

Give an example of something you have recently **investigated** in science class.

2 min.	3 min.
1. Turn and talk to your partner or group.	**2.** Write 2–4 sentences.
Use this space to take notes or draw your ideas.	Be ready to share what you have written.

Study the definitions of the words. Then do the exercises that follow.

abdicate
ab´ di kāt

v. To give up a high office.
When Edward VIII **abdicated** the throne in 1936, his younger brother became king of England.

assume
ə so͞om´

v. 1. To take for granted; to suppose.
We cannot **assume** that Mom and Dad will meet us at the station if the train is two hours late.

2. To take over; to occupy.
Ruth Bader Ginsberg **assumed** office as a justice of the Supreme Court in 1993.

3. To pretend to have.
Edin **assumed** a look of innocence when Vilma asked who had eaten the rest of the salad.

Tell your partner what lunch you assume you will eat tomorrow.

bungle
buŋ´ gəl

v. To do something badly or without skill.
Because the shortstop **bungled** the double play, the runner made it safely to first base.

dominate
däm´ ə nāt

v. 1. To rule or control; to have a very important place or position.
Rock **dominated** popular music in America for several decades.

2. To rise high above.
The Willis Tower **dominates** the Chicago skyline.

Talk to your partner about a team that dominates its sport.

former
fôr´ mər

adj. Coming before in time; having been at an earlier time.
Three **former** mayors were invited to the dedication of our new city hall.

n. The first of two just mentioned.
Both the crocodile and the alligator are dangerous, but the **former** is more aggressive.

guardian
gär´ dē ən

n. 1. One who protects.
This ferocious dog acts as **guardian** of the property at night.

2. One who legally has the care of another person.
You need the permission of your parent or **guardian** to go on field trips.

hoist hoist	*v.* To lift or raise, especially by using a rope. The sailors **hoisted** the sails as we left the harbor. *n.* Something used to lift, as a crane or pulley. We cannot raise this heavy machine without a **hoist.**
intercept in tər sept´ 	*v.* To stop or seize something while it is on its way somewhere. The Coast Guard can **intercept** boats in United States waters to investigate their cargoes. *Discuss with your partner why a teacher might intercept a note being passed in class.*
jubilee jo͞o´ bə lē	*n.* The celebration of an anniversary, especially a fiftieth anniversary or beyond. The school marked its **jubilee** with a banquet for graduates from the past fifty years.
kin kin	*adj.* Related by birth or marriage. Are you **kin** to the Jordans, or are you just a friend of theirs? *n. pl.* (also **kinfolk**) Relatives; family. She celebrated her ninetieth birthday with all her **kin** around her. **next of kin** The person most closely related to someone. The hospital requires the name of your **next of kin** when you are admitted.
pardon pärd´n 	*v.* 1. To forgive. Alice **pardoned** the Red Queen's rude remark. 2. To free from legal punishment. The president of the United States has the power to **pardon** those convicted of crimes. *n.* The act of forgiving or freeing from legal punishment. The president granted a **pardon** to the man who showed many years of good behavior. *Tell your partner why you should pardon a friend who says something mean to you.*
proclaim prō klām´	*v.* To make known publicly; to announce. The mayor **proclaimed** May 18 a city holiday.

provoke
prō vōk´

v. 1. To annoy or make angry.
Cho said he took Katie's toys away because she **provoked** him with her constant talking.

2. To call forth; to rouse.
Senator Rodriguez's comments **provoked** laughter in the audience.

provocative *adj.* (prə väk´ ə tiv) Calling forth anger, amusement, or thoughtfulness; trying to cause a response.
You were being **provocative** when you kept asking the same question over and over.

Say something funny to provoke laughter from your partner.

---

reign
rān

v. 1. To rule as a queen or king.
King Hussein of Jordan **reigned** for over forty years.

2. To be widespread.
Terror **reigned** in the streets of Paris during the French Revolution.

n. 1. The rule of a queen or king; the time during which a person rules.
The American Revolution occurred during the **reign** of George III.

Discuss with your partner whether you can focus on schoolwork when noise reigns in your home.

---

riot
rī´ ət

n. 1. Public disorder or violence.
Good citizens did all they could to prevent **riots** after the local team lost in the playoffs.

2. A great and seemingly disordered quantity of something.
My dad's rose garden is a **riot** of color in the summer.

v. To take part in a disorder.
As the crowd of townspeople **rioted,** leaders tried to calm the situation.

Tell your partner about a place that is a riot of sounds, such as the zoo or a fair.

Read the following sentences. If the word in bold is used correctly, write C on the line. If the word is used incorrectly, write I on the line.

1. (a) The **bungle** was delivered on Tuesday. _____
   (b) They built the playground so fast, they **bungled** it pretty badly. _____
   (c) Somebody **bungled** the order, and now we have way too many pencils. _____
   (d) I **bungled** everything up and put it in storage. _____

2. (a) I was able to **hoist** myself up the rope and into the tree house. _____
   (b) We **hoisted** the flag and watched it flutter in the breeze. _____
   (c) The book club is **hoisting** a party for the new members. _____
   (d) We need a **hoist** to lift this boulder. _____

3. (a) The Roman Empire **reigned** from 27 BCE to 476 CE. _____
   (b) The **reign** of England's Queen Elizabeth II began in 1952. _____
   (c) The driver took the **reigns** and told the horse to stop. _____
   (d) Hope **reigned** in the school as students waited to hear if they could go home early. _____

4. (a) The governor can grant a **pardon** to someone convicted of a crime. _____
   (b) "**Pardon** my interruption," he said, "but are you finished yet?" _____
   (c) William **pardoned** everyone for coming. _____
   (d) **Pardon** the lunch before you sit down. _____

5. (a) He **provoked** a funny story about a clown. _____
   (b) My little brother is being **provocative** with his stomping and won't be quiet. _____
   (c) Your insults **provoked** Emily into anger. _____
   (d) My money had been **provoked.** _____

6. (a) The fire chief said the house was **proclaimed** in the fire. _____
   (b) On January 1, 1863, Abraham Lincoln **proclaimed** the end of slavery. _____
   (c) The first settlers started **proclaiming** for gold in 1849. _____
   (d) Mel **proclaimed** that she would no longer go to dance class. _____

7. (a) Mr. Jackson will **assume** the office of mayor on January 1. ____
(b) Binh **assumed** a hurt look, but we knew he was laughing inside. ____
(c) We **assume** traffic will be heavy, so we should leave early. ____
(d) A'kierra **assumed** me that the party was not her idea. ____

8. (a) Her paintings are a **riot** of blues, greens, and oranges. ____
(b) The **riot** ended quickly, and no serious injuries were reported. ____
(c) Though many people **rioted,** it was those who spoke calmly who made the most difference. ____
(d) I **rioted** quietly as I climbed the stairs to my bedroom. ____

9. (a) Muhammad Ali **dominated** the sport of boxing in the 1960s. ____
(b) The Freedom Tower **dominates** the New York skyline. ____
(c) The robot is **dominated** once you push the green button. ____
(d) Here are the people who have been **dominated** for the student council. ____

10. (a) There's an **intercepting** story online. ____
(b) The note was **intercepted** by the teacher, who was not happy. ____
(c) Suki keeps **intercepting** me whenever I try to talk. ____
(d) The pass was **intercepted** by the home team, who went on to score. ____

abdicate
assume
bungle
dominate
former
guardian
hoist
intercept
jubilee
kin
pardon
proclaim
provoke
reign
riot

Making Connections

Circle the letter next to each correct answer. There may be more than one correct answer.

1. Which word or words go with *give up?*
   (a) abdicate   (b) assume   (c) provoke   (d) yield

2. Which word or words go with *earlier time?*
   (a) former   (b) duration   (c) previous   (d) delicate

3. Which word or words go with *protect?*
   (a) guardian   (b) bungle   (c) reign   (d) pardon

4. Which word or words go with *special occasion?*
   (a) riot   (b) jubilee   (c) celebrate   (d) provoke

5. Which word or words go with *family?*
   (a) ancestor   (b) kinfolk   (c) bungle   (d) intercept

6. Which word or words go with *disorder?*
   (a) rebellion   (b) transformation
   (c) illumination   (d) riot

7. Which word or words go with *give up office?*
   (a) employ   (b) reign   (c) abdicate   (d) riot

8. Which word or words go with *forgive?*
   (a) dominate   (b) intercept   (c) employ   (d) pardon

9. Which word or words go with *make known?*
   (a) assume   (b) intercept   (c) provoke   (d) proclaim

10. Which word or words go with *higher?*
    (a) collapse   (b) elevate   (c) escalate   (d) hoist

16c Determining Meanings

Circle the letter next to each answer choice that correctly completes the sentence. There may be more than one correct answer.

1. We **intercepted**
   (a) the package before it could be delivered.
   (b) the ball after the game began.
   (c) ourselves between the two dogs.
   (d) the other team before the game began.

2. The **abdication**
   (a) was put in an envelope and mailed.
   (b) of the queen after fifteen years was shocking.
   (c) of the light bulb was amazing.
   (d) of the presidential office to the vice president happened quickly.

3. The **kinfolk**
   (a) lasted just a short while, and then it was over.
   (b) gathered around the table.
   (c) are all invited to the big family birthday party.
   (d) is kept in the barn until we can clean the stall.

4. What **provoked**
   (a) such an aggressive response?
   (b) Santos to challenge Hernandez to a game of basketball?
   (c) Hermione in the hand?
   (d) the disease was a bite from a tick.

5. The **assumption**
   (a) that he could get away with it was unbelievable.
   (b) is that if she studies enough, she will pass the test.
   (c) of ice into water will happen more quickly in the sun.
   (d) is that the weather will clear up.

6. Her **formerly**
   (a) letter is addressed to the president.
   (b) old bike has been fixed up like new!
   (c) dress is ready to wear.
   (d) sad face is now happy.

abdicate
assume
bungle
dominate
former
guardian
hoist
intercept
jubilee
kin
pardon
proclaim
provoke
reign
riot

7. He **dominated**
   (a) the weight-lifting competition by showing superior strength.
   (b) the honey by first finding the beehive.
   (c) the Spanish words into English.
   (d) the room with his loud voice, which annoyed everyone else.

8. We **bungled**
   (a) our chance to win by not working as a team.
   (b) the quiz because we didn't study.
   (c) and danced gracefully on the stage.
   (d) my mom into letting us go inside.

Completing Sentences

Complete the sentences to demonstrate your knowledge of the words in bold.

1. I **assume** that

   _____.

2. One animal that would **dominate** an elephant's height would be a

   _____.

3. If you **pardon** someone, that means you

   _____.

4. Something a teacher might **proclaim** is:

   _____.

5. Someone who **reigns** might be a

   _____.

6. My **former** teacher's name was

   _____.

7. I'm sure I would **bungle** it if I tried to

   _____.

8. The name of one of my **kin** is

   _____.

9. Something that is a **riot** of color is

_____.

10. A **provocative** statement might be:

_____.

16E Vocabulary in Context
Read the passage.

The Last Queen of the Islands

Although she never dreamed it would happen, Liliuokalani grew up to become the queen of the Hawaiian Islands. Born on the island of Oahu in 1838, she was in her teens when her parents died. Her older brother Kalakaua became her **guardian.** They were **kin** to the Hawaiian royal family, but Kalakaua was not expected to succeed to the throne.

When King Lunalilo died in 1874, after ruling for barely one year, many believed that Queen Emma, widow of a **former** king, would be chosen to succeed him. It came as a surprise to Queen Emma's supporters that the elected members of Hawaii's governing body passed her by and **proclaimed** Kalakaua king instead.

King Kalakaua **reigned** for seventeen years. The islands were **dominated** at that time by powerful planters and businessmen. Chief among them was Sanford Dole. Dole was a lawyer, a politician, and the planters' natural leader. In 1887, this group forced Kalakaua to sign away almost all of his powers. That made him Hawaii's ruler in name only. Kalakaua had no children; following the death of his younger brother in 1877, he chose Liliuokalani to succeed him to the throne. She ruled in her brother's place when he was absent from the kingdom. She also represented him at Queen Victoria's Golden **Jubilee** in London in 1887.

Liliuokalani ascended the throne of Hawaii following her brother's death in 1891. She promptly set about regaining real power. The Hawaiian people resented the takeover of their government by the _haoles_, as the white-skinned Americans are called in Hawaiian. They supported their queen. Liliuokalani declared a plan for government that gave more power to native Hawaiians. The haoles formed a committee to stop her. On January 16,

| abdicate |
| assume |
| bungle |
| dominate |
| former |
| guardian |
| hoist |
| intercept |
| jubilee |
| kin |
| pardon |
| proclaim |
| provoke |
| reign |
| riot |

1893, the haole leaders brought in American sailors and marines who were stationed on nearby ships. They were there to prevent **riots** from breaking out in support of the queen.

The next day, the committee of haoles set up its own government with Sanford Dole as leader. Liliuokalani opposed this. She asked the president of the United States for help. After an investigation, President Grover Cleveland ordered that Liliuokalani be returned to power. But Dole claimed that the U.S. government had no right to interfere in Hawaii's affairs. On July 4, 1894, he **assumed** the presidency of the new Republic of Hawaii. Liliuokalani remained queen, but with no power to govern.

Early the next year, a group of Liliuokalani's supporters rebelled against the new government. The attempt was badly **bungled,** failing miserably. Dole accused Liliuokalani of **provoking** it and arrested her. She steadfastly denied being involved. But messages between her and her followers had been **intercepted,** and weapons were found in her home. Liliuokalani was told that if she would **abdicate,** her supporters, who were then in jail, would not be put to death. To save their lives, she agreed to step down. She was sentenced to five years imprisonment for her role in the revolt. After eight months Dole **pardoned** her on the condition that she take no further part in politics. Liliuokalani withdrew to her home, where she continued to fly the Hawaiian flag.

In 1898, Hawaii became part of the United States, with Sanford Dole serving as governor. For many years, Liliuokalani brought lawsuits against the United States to seek compensation for the injustice of stealing Hawaii from its people. Then, in 1917, during World War I, the first Hawaiians died fighting for the United States against Germany. The day she received the news, Liliuokalani lowered the Hawaiian flag and **hoisted** the Stars and Stripes.

▶ **Answer each of the following questions with a sentence. If a question does not contain a vocabulary word from the lesson's word list, use one in your answer. Use each word only once.**

1. What do you think was the significance of Liliuokalani's **hoisting** the Stars and Stripes?

_____

_____

2. What is the meaning of **guardian** as it is used in the passage?

_____

_____

3. What did Queen Emma expect to happen when Lunalilo died?

_____

_____

4. Why didn't Liliuokalani think about becoming queen of the Hawaiian Islands when she was a young girl?

_____

_____

5. Why was Queen Emma a very strong choice for ruler of Hawaii in 1874?

_____

_____

6. Why did Liliuokalani visit London in 1887?

_____

_____

7. Why couldn't President Cleveland **dominate** Sanford Dole?

_____

_____

8. Why were American sailors and marines brought to land in January 1893?

_____

_____

9. Why was Liliuokalani's situation difficult when she was asked to **abdicate?**

_____

_____

10. What is the meaning of **assumed** as it is used in the passage?

_____

_____

11. Why did Dole's government continue to rule after the rebellion of 1895?

_____

_____

abdicate
assume
bungle
dominate
former
guardian
hoist
intercept
jubilee
kin
pardon
proclaim
provoke
reign
riot

12. Why did the *haoles* claim that Liliuokalani took part in the 1895 uprising?

_____

_____

13. How did Liliuokalani respond when accused of being responsible for the 1895 rebellion?

_____

_____

14. What is the meaning of **pardoned** as it is used in the passage?

_____

_____

15. How many years was Liliuokalani queen before Hawaii became a republic?

_____

_____

Fun & Fascinating FACTS

- The antonym of **former** is *latter*. If given a choice between silk and cotton, and you choose the *latter*, you will get cotton. If you choose the **former**, you will get silk.

- The Latin prefix *inter-* means "between." *Inter*national affairs are those conducted *between* nations; *inter*state commerce is business conducted *between* states. This prefix is combined with the root from the Latin verb *capere*, "to take," to form the word **intercept**. Something that is *intercepted* is *taken* as it passes *between* the sender and the receiver.

- **Jubilee** comes from the Hebrew *yobhel*, which was a ram's horn used as a trumpet. It was blown every fifty years to celebrate the release of the Jewish people from bondage.

The word applies especially to a fiftieth anniversary but is used to mark other anniversaries as well. In 1897, Queen Victoria celebrated her Diamond **Jubilee**, by which time she had occupied the British throne for sixty years.

- Homophones usually come in pairs but sometimes come in threes. **Reign**, *rain*, and *rein* are homophones. To rein in a horse is to control its speed by pulling on the reins.

assume

verb 1. To think something is true, even if you don't have proof.

2. To take over control of something.

Context Clues

These sentences give clues to the meaning of **assume.**

> *Jaden didn't see Hope's bicycle at school, so he **assumed** she wasn't there yet.*
>
> *Ms. Martinez will **assume** the role of principal at the beginning of August.*

Discussion & Writing Prompt

What would you **assume** if you saw a person wearing a bathing suit and carrying a beach towel?

2 min.	3 min.
1. Turn and talk to your partner or group.	**2.** Write 2–4 sentences.
Use this space to take notes or draw your ideas.	Be ready to share what you have written.

Review

Crossword Puzzle   Solve the crossword puzzle by studying the clues and filling in the answer boxes. The number after a clue is the lesson the word is from.

Clues Across

1. To fall over (15)
5. Able to be seen; within view (13)
9. Upset or angry
10. A violent public disorder (16)
11. Something that causes great damage (15)
13. To run from danger (15)
14. To make known publicly (16)
17. To say what will happen before it takes place (15)
23. To seize something while it is on its way (16)
25. One who protects (16)
26. To have
27. Opposite of *in front of*
28. Worn to protect the head
29. New Year's _____

Clues Down

2. To make angry (16)
3. Opposite of *begin*
4. To take for granted (16)
6. Showing great depth of feeling (15)
7. To hire and put to work for pay (14)
8. To do nothing (14)
10. A small wave (13)
12. To need (14)
15. A partner in business (14)
16. To stick out (13)
18. The rule of a queen or king (16)
19. A tasty tidbit (13)
20. A person who is not yet an adult (15)
21. A ten-year period (14)
22. To move suddenly and unexpectedly (15)
24. To become less wide at one end (13)

Study the definitions of the words. Then do the exercises that follow.

afflict
ə flikt´

v. To bring or cause pain and suffering.
The patient has been **afflicted** with swollen feet for several months.

affliction *n.* A condition of pain, suffering, or trouble.
Frida Kahlo's **affliction** was the result of a serious accident.

barren
bār´ ən

adj. Not fruitful; not reproducing.
When the topsoil is washed away, the land is **barren.**

consist
kən sist´

v. To be made up; to contain.
The wedding banquet will **consist** of many dishes from India.

Tell your partner what your breakfast today consisted of.

drought
drout

n. A long period without rain.
The poor harvest was due to the **drought.**

erode
ē rōd´

v. To wear away bit by bit; to wear away by action of wind, water, or ice.
Heavy seas from yesterday's storm have **eroded** parts of the cliff.

erosion *n.* The process or state of eroding.
Cutting down many trees in one area leads to soil **erosion.**

Show your partner what you would sound like if your tongue had eroded away in your mouth.

expand
ek spand´

v. 1. To make or become larger.
You can **expand** your chest by taking a very deep breath.

2. To give further details of.
Mr. da Silva asked me to **expand** on some of the information in my report.

expansion *n.* The act, process, or result of enlarging.
The lunchroom **expansion** will allow our school to offer more food choices.

Explain to your partner how to make a balloon expand.

famine
fam´ in

n. A widespread and long-lasting shortage of food that may cause starvation.
The **famine** in Somalia was the result of several poor harvests in a row.

fertile	*adj.* 1. Able to produce good crops.
furt´ l	The major reason we grow such large tomatoes is the **fertile** soil.
	2. Able to produce offspring.
	A female cat is **fertile** at six months.
	3. Able to produce ideas; inventive.
	Many ideas sprang from Thomas Edison's **fertile** brain.

oasis	*n.* A place where there is water in an otherwise dry area.
ō ā´ sis	**oases** *n. pl.* (ō ā´ sēz)
	Travelers across the Sahara try to reach the next **oasis** before nightfall.

pasture	*n.* A field of growing grass where animals can eat; a meadow.
pas´ chər	We put the sheep in a different **pasture** to give the grass in this one a chance to grow back.
	v. To put animals out in a field to eat grass.
	We **pasture** our horses on a neighbor's land.

primitive	*adj.* 1. From earliest times; ancient.
prim´ i tiv	The **primitive** cave drawings are over fifteen thousand years old.
	2. Simple or crude.
	We are proud of the **primitive** racecar we built for the school race.

....

Chat with your partner about why a preschool child's drawings look primitive.

refuge	n. 1. Shelter or protection from harm.
ref´ yōōj	The hikers found **refuge** from the blizzard in a nearby cave.
	2. A place of safety.
	During the hurricane, families living in beach houses found **refuge** in the high school gym.
	refugee *n.* A person forced to leave her or his home or country to seek protection from danger.
	A camp for Kurdish **refugees** was set up between Turkey and Iraq.

....

Tell your partner where your family might find refuge if the electricity went out at home.

| **revert** | *v.* To go back to an earlier condition, often one that is not as satisfactory. |
| rē vurt´ | During the week that the electric power lines were being repaired, we **reverted** to eating our meals by candlelight. |

....

Talk with your partner about what would happen if we reverted back to writing letters instead of e-mails or texts.

teem	*v.* To be filled; to occur in large numbers.
tēm	The Columbia River once **teemed** with salmon.

Show your partner how you would act in a place that teems with bugs.

wither	*v.* To become dried out; to lose freshness.
wi*th*´ ər	The crops will **wither** unless we have rain soon.

17A Finding Meanings

Choose two phrases to form a sentence that correctly uses a word from Word List 17. Then write the sentence.

1. (a) go beyond what is permitted.   (c) To erode is to
   (b) To expand is to   (d) gradually wear away.

   _____

   _____

2. (a) a place with water in an otherwise dry area.   (c) An oasis is
   (b) a condition from which one suffers.   (d) A pasture is

   _____

   _____

3. (a) give more details about it.   (c) To revert to something is to
   (b) To expand on something is to   (d) mention it for the first time.

   _____

   _____

4. (a) To consist of something is to   (c) be made up of it.
   (b) To teem with something is to   (d) be associated with it.

   _____

   _____

afflict
barren
consist
drought
erode
expand
famine
fertile
oasis
pasture
primitive
refuge
revert
teem
wither

5. (a) To wither is to   (c) go back to an earlier condition.
   (b) continue to improve.   (d) To revert is to

_____

_____

6. (a) a place of safety in time of   (c) A drought is
       danger.
   (b) a grassy area where   (d) A pasture is
       animals feed.

_____

_____

7. (a) To wither is to   (c) dry out from lack of water.
   (b) To teem is to   (d) sink to a lower level.

_____

_____

8. (a) A famine is   (c) a long period without rain.
   (b) A drought is   (d) an area where little can grow.

_____

_____

9. (a) An expansion is   (c) An affliction is
   (b) a place of great danger.   (d) a condition causing suffering.

_____

_____

10. (a) A refuge is   (c) a person in poor health.
    (b) a place of safety.   (d) A famine is

_____

_____

Just the Right Word

Replace each phrase in bold with a single word (or form of the word) from the word list.

1. Al Kufrah is a well-known **place where water is found in an otherwise dry area** in Libya.

2. When children taunted her, it led to the **gradual wearing away** of her confidence.

3. The way the villagers draw water from the river may be **the same as that used in very early times,** but it is quite effective.

4. If the cow you bought is not **capable of producing calves,** the dealer will return the money you paid for it.

5. Our breakfast usually **is made up** of cereal, milk, fruit, and juice.

6. Because the number of children taking tennis lessons is **growing larger** every year, we now offer three sessions during the summer.

7. Acid rain destroys lakes that once **were filled** with fish.

8. President Roosevelt was **made to suffer when he came down** with polio at the age of thirty-nine.

9. We **provide grass for** our goats in a neighbor's field.

10. Many **persons fleeing for their safety** from Nazi Germany came to the United States in the 1930s.

afflict
barren
consist
drought
erode
expand
famine
fertile
oasis
pasture
primitive
refuge
revert
teem
wither

Applying Meanings

Circle the letter or letters next to each correct answer. There may be more than one correct answer.

1. Which of the following might **wither?**
   (a) crops
   (b) trees
   (c) leaves
   (d) beaches

2. Which of the following could one **expand?**
   (a) one's knowledge
   (b) one's age
   (c) one's home
   (d) one's chest

3. Which of the following can result from **famine?**
   (a) despair
   (b) sickness
   (c) death
   (d) hunger

4. Which of the following can be **barren?**
   (a) a goat
   (b) a valley
   (c) a pear tree
   (d) a pasture

5. Which of the following might occur during a **drought?**
   (a) restrictions on water use
   (b) forest fires
   (c) a yearning for rain
   (d) flooding

6. Which of the following can be **fertile?**
   (a) a kitten
   (b) soil
   (c) a mind
   (d) a morsel

7. Which of the following might one find in a **pasture?**
   (a) cargo
   (b) cows
   (c) sheep
   (d) grass

8. Which of the following can be **eroded?**
   (a) soil
   (b) confidence
   (c) cliffs
   (d) savings

17D Word Study: Homophones

Read the pairs of sentences. Then choose the word that best completes each sentence.

Words that sound the same but have different meanings and/or spellings are called **homophones.**

idol / idle

1. We didn't _____, as we wanted to finish our chores quickly.

2. The _____ was made of gold with rubies for its eyes.

taper / tapir

3. The _____ was dripping wax onto the table.

4. The _____ is an animal with a long, flexible snout.

teem / team

5. The streets _____ with tourists during the summer months.

6. May the best _____ win.

reigns / reins

7. The chart lists the _____ of all the English kings and queens.

8. The _____ are used to control the horse.

barren / baron

9. The Sahara is _____ except for the occasional oasis.

10. A _____ can sit in the British House of Lords.

minor / miner

11. In the U.S., anyone under eighteen is considered a _____.

12. Every gold _____ in California hoped to strike it rich.

flee / flea

13. A _____ can jump many times its height.

14. Most people were able to _____ inland before the hurricane struck.

afflict
barren
consist
drought
erode
expand
famine
fertile
oasis
pasture
primitive
refuge
revert
teem
wither

hanger / hangar

15. The aircraft was wheeled out of the _____ .

16. I put the coat on a _____ and hung it in the closet.

17E Vocabulary in Context

Read the passage.

A Harvest of Sand

The ability of the earth to support life depends on the amount of rainfall it receives. The tropical rain forests of Africa, Asia, and Central and South America are **teeming** with life. They get up to four hundred inches of rain a year. Yet in other parts of the world, little or no rain falls, making the land **barren.** Areas where the annual rainfall is less than ten inches a year are called deserts.

The largest of the earth's deserts is the Sahara, in northern Africa. The Sahara covers an area almost as big as the United States. Apart from the central portion, which is mountainous, the Sahara **consists** mostly of sand. There is water, but it lies far below the surface in ancient underground lakes. In some places it bubbles to the surface in the form of springs. More often, though, wells have to be dug to get to it. In these places the soil is **fertile,** and people can grow crops and raise animals. **Oases** spring up around these places, often becoming the size of small towns. They are a welcome sight to the travelers who cross this harsh land on the backs of camels, or, more commonly today, in four-wheel-drive vehicles.

South of the Sahara are the countries that make up the Sahel. The Sahel is an area that stretches four thousand miles, from Senegal in the west to Ethiopia in the east. This part of Africa was once mostly grassland. As grassland, it provided good **pasture** for cattle and made it possible for the people of these countries to be reasonably well fed. In recent years, however, it has been **afflicted** with long dry spells. They have been the worst ones in nearly two centuries. As the **droughts** continue, rivers and lakes dry up; without water, the grass **withers** and the cattle are left with nothing to feed on. To make matters worse, too many trees that held the soil in place have been cut down for firewood. This has resulted in widespread soil **erosion.**

Because of changing weather patterns, the Sahara is spreading into the Sahel. As it continues to **expand** southward, the Sahara has taken over more than a quarter of a million square miles since the 1950s. This is equivalent to an area roughly the size of France and Austria combined. Although nothing can be done to change weather patterns, scientists believe that in time conditions will change. If that happens, the land that is now desert may **revert** to grassland.

The people of the Sahel have suffered greatly, however. Hundreds of thousands have already died as a result of **famine.** One third of all the children born in the Sahel still die before their fifth birthdays. Millions have left their once prosperous villages and have poured into the overcrowded cities to the south, where they live in **primitive** shelters. Nouakchott, on Africa's west coast, was home to fifteen thousand people in the 1950s. Accurate counts are hard to come by in this part of Africa, but a 2016 estimate put the figure as high as two million, most of them **refugees** from the slowly spreading desert to the north.

▶ **Answer each of the following questions with a sentence. If a question does not contain a vocabulary word from the lesson's word list, use one in your answer. Use each word only once.**

afflict
barren
consist
drought
erode
expand
famine
fertile
oasis
pasture
primitive
refuge
revert
teem
wither

1. Why are deserts **barren** places?

_____

_____

2. What happens to the people of the Sahel who are driven from their land?

_____

_____

3. Where is it possible to grow crops in the Sahara, and why?

_____

_____

4. How has the Sahara changed in recent years?

_____

_____

5. What is the meaning of **fertile** as it is used in the passage?

_____

_____

6. In what way do tropical rain forests differ from deserts?

_____

_____

7. What is the main cause of **drought** in the Sahel?

_____

_____

8. What is the meaning of **primitive** as it is used in the passage?

_____

_____

9. How are cattle affected by the worsening conditions in the Sahel?

_____

_____

10. What happens to plants that don't get enough water?

_____

_____

11. Why does the cutting down of trees lead to soil **erosion?**

_____

_____

12. Why do scientists think the Sahel may not remain a desert?

_____

_____

13. How does the present dry spell in the Sahel compare with those in the past?

_____

_____

14. Why would the Sahara have a brownish color when seen from space?

_____

_____

15. How can food shipments from outside help the people of the Sahel?

_____

_____

Fun & Fascinating FACTS

- To **afflict** is to cause pain and suffering. To *inflict* (Word List 6) is to cause something damaging or painful to be felt. If you are confused by the similarity in meaning of these two words, you are not alone. The difference between them is that **afflict** deals with what is *felt,* whereas *inflict* deals with what is *done.* In the sentence "The judge *inflicted* a severe sentence," the judge *did* something. In the sentence "The prisoner was *afflicted* with guilt," the prisoner *felt* something.

- **Barren** and *baron* are homophones. A *baron* is a nobleman. It was the English barons who, in 1215, forced King John to sign the Magna Carta, granting civil rights to English citizens.

- **Teem** and *team* form another pair of homophones. A team is a group of people who play or work together.

- **Primitive** tools, which may be tens of thousand of years old, are found buried in many parts of the world. They are among the first tools made by humans, as the word *primitive* suggests. It comes from the Latin *primus,* which means "first." A number of other English words share this root. A *primary* reason is one that comes *first* in importance; a *primer* is a book of *first* instruction in a subject; and a *prime* minister in many countries is the leader who is *first* in importance.

- **Wither,** a verb, should not be confused with the adverb *whither,* meaning "to what place; where." These two words are not homophones, because the "h" in *whither* is sounded. *Whither* is a poetic word that is falling out of use. Once when people wished to know where someone was going, they would ask, "Whither are you going?" or "Whither goest thou?"

afflict

barren

consist

drought

erode

expand

famine

fertile

oasis

pasture

primitive

refuge

revert

teem

wither

expand

verb 1. To spread out or become larger; to make something become larger.

2. To give more details.

. . . .

Word Family

expandable (adjective)
expanding (verb)
expansion (noun)

Phrasal Verbs

expand upon When you **expand upon** something, you give more details about it.

> *Her friends were listening closely, so Alicia **expanded upon** her story about rescuing her cat from a tree.*

Discussion & Writing Prompt

How can a house be **expanded?**

`2 min.`	`3 min.`
1. Turn and talk to your partner or group.	2. Write 2–4 sentences.
Use this space to take notes or draw your ideas.	Be ready to share what you have written.

Study the definitions of the words. Then do the exercises that follow.

animated
an´ ə mãt əd

adj. 1. Alive or seeming to be alive.
The movie combines **animated** cartoon figures with live actors.

2. Full of energy; lively.
The class discussion became quite **animated** when we talked about raising the driving age.

Show your partner how you can be animated while still sitting in your seat.

betray
bē trã´

v. 1. To be disloyal to.
Members of the Underground Railroad could be counted on not to **betray** enslaved people to the people who tried to capture them.

2. To show; to reveal.
Jonas insisted that he wasn't upset, but his tears **betrayed** his true feelings.

Discuss with your partner a situation when you might not want to betray your real feelings.

convince
kən vins´

v. To make someone feel sure or certain; to persuade.
I tried to **convince** my parents that I was old enough to be left alone in the house.

decline
dē klīn´

v. 1. To slope or pass to a lower level.
The path **declines** sharply here, then rises.

2. To refuse to accept.
Olga **declined** my offer of a ride to school because she wanted to walk.

3. To become less or weaker.
My brother's health could **decline** if he does not eat a variety of good foods.

n. 1. A change to a smaller amount or lower level.
The **decline** in attendance at the ballpark worries the team's owners.

2. A loss of strength or power.
The **decline** of our town stopped when new businesses moved in.

Take turns with your partner asking each other to do something. Politely decline your partner's invitation.

hilarious
hi lar´ ē əs

adj. Very funny.
The comedian's **hilarious** jokes had us all laughing.

| **likeness** | *n.* The state of being similar; something that is similar. |
| līk´ nəs | Your **likeness** to your sister is remarkable. |

| **meager** | *adj.* Poor in quality or insufficient in amount. |
| mē´ gər | A stale crust of bread makes a **meager** meal. |

| **mischief** | *n.* 1. Harm or damage. |
| mis´ chif | Our neighbor's meddling in other people's affairs caused a lot of **mischief.** |

2. Behavior that causes harm or trouble.
Their **mischief** during class will get them in trouble.

3. Playfulness; harmless amusement.
Hiding her mother's hat was just the child's **mischief.**

mischievous *adj.* (mis´ chə vəs) Playful in a naughty way.
The **mischievous** cat pawed at the dog's tail.

| **negotiate** | *v.* 1. To arrange by talking over. |
| ni gō´ shē āt | When my parents disagree over what to eat for dinner, they **negotiate** a compromise. |

2. To travel successfully along or over.
This slope has some difficult sections that only accomplished hikers can **negotiate.**

Demonstrate for your partner how you negotiate a crowded hallway or sidewalk.

| **obsolete** | *adj.* No longer sold or in wide use because it is out-of-date. |
| äb sə lēt´ | Digital music players have made CDs nearly **obsolete.** |

| **retain** | *v.* 1. To hold on to; to keep possession of. |
| rē tān´ | Because of today's victory, we **retained** our position at the top of the girls' hockey league. |

2. To hire the services of.
Our school has **retained** a crossing guard who makes sure students cross the street safely.

Discuss with your partner what things you would like to retain if you were asked to donate all but three of your belongings.

sensation
sen sā´ shən

n. 1. A feeling that comes from stimulation of the senses.
Drinking hot cocoa after two hours of sledding gave us a warm **sensation.**

2. A feeling of great interest or excitement or the cause of such a feeling.
The appearance at our school of the basketball star caused a **sensation.**

sensational *adj.* 1. Causing great curiosity and interest.
The **sensational** headline led me to buy the newspaper.

2. Very great or excellent.
With your quick mind, you'll make a **sensational** addition to the debating team.

Describe for your partner what the sensation of a sunburn or rash is like.

somber
säm´ bər

adj. 1. Dark; gloomy.
We began our hike under a **somber** sky; fortunately, the sun came out in the afternoon.

2. Sad; serious.
News from the ongoing wars put us in a **somber** mood.

subsequent
sub´ sə kwənt

adj. Coming later; following.
The first book in the series was a disappointment, but **subsequent** ones have been very enjoyable.

Talk to your partner about what happens subsequent to dropping an egg out of the window.

vow
vou

v. To promise seriously.
The rescue workers **vowed** to continue working until all those trapped in the building were freed.

n. A pledge; a promise.
When my parents became citizens of the United States, they made a **vow** to support this country.

18A Using Words in Context

Read the following sentences. If the word in bold is used correctly, write C on the line. If the word is used incorrectly, write I on the line.

1. (a) The car chase provides a **sensational** ending to the movie. _____
   (b) I felt a tingling **sensation** in my foot. _____
   (c) The birth of the triplet polar bears was the **sensation** of the year. _____
   (d) The water grew more **sensational** as the storm approached. _____

2. (a) The false rumors caused a lot of **mischief** in the classroom. _____
   (b) My sister was just being **mischievous** and didn't mean to hurt anyone. _____
   (c) The heavy rain turned the mud **mischievous.** _____
   (d) I pressed the **mischief** over my sweaty forehead. _____

3. (a) The teacher grew more and more **animated** as he taught. _____
   (b) She was very **animated** as she slept soundly and quietly. _____
   (c) My favorite **animated** movie is on TV tonight. _____
   (d) Ravi sat on the **animated** stone bench. _____

4. (a) The **decline** in the number of Asian elephants is causing concern. _____
   (b) She ran up the **decline** as fast as she could. _____
   (c) A steep **decline** led to the water's edge. _____
   (d) I had to **decline** the offer. _____

5. (a) My parents **retained** someone to paint our house. _____
   (b) If Marcus moves away, we will no longer **retain** the title of best baseball team. _____
   (c) I want to **retain** as much of my pizza as I can to eat later. _____
   (d) The swimmer **retained** his breath while underwater. _____

6. (a) Three is **subsequent** to two. _____
   (b) My aunt wasn't home last month, but I saw her on a **subsequent** visit. _____
   (c) He **subsequently** denied that he said he would be there. _____
   (d) Deidre became quite **subsequent** after she got to know us. _____

7. (a) I was mad about the **meager** portions at the restaurant. ____
   (b) She was feeling a bit **meager,** so she went to lie down. ____
   (c) We were eager for the **meager** bits of information that slowly started
       to come. ____
   (d) I received a **meager** fifteen presents for my birthday. ____

8. (a) Ashanti became **convinced** that bees were following her. ____
   (b) My uncle **convinced** his shoes before he came down the stairs. ____
   (c) The principal **convinced** the parents that she knew what she was
       doing. ____
   (d) **Convince** the hot cocoa before you drink it, please. ____

9. (a) A **hilarious** movie usually makes people sad. ____
   (b) Be careful of the wet floor when you walk because it's **hilarious.** ____
   (c) I couldn't stop laughing, because the show was so **hilarious.** ____
   (d) Akbar always tells the most **hilarious** stories. ____

10. (a) Timone was **obsolete** that he couldn't go to the party. ____
    (b) The older skateboard is **obsolete** and has been replaced with the
        new model. ____
    (c) Arti said her relationship with her best friend is **obsolete.** ____
    (d) The automobile made horse-drawn travel **obsolete.** ____

animated
betray
convince
decline
hilarious
likeness
meager
mischief
negotiate
obsolete
retain
sensation
somber
subsequent
vow

Making Connections

Circle the letter next to each correct answer. There may be more than one correct answer.

1. Which word or words go with *reveal?*
   (a) forsake   (b) retain   (c) assume   (d) betray

2. Which word or words go with *the same?*
   (a) sensation   (b) likeness   (c) mischief   (d) equivalent

3. Which word or words go with *compromise?*
   (a) negotiate   (b) retain   (c) decline   (d) intercept

4. Which word or words go with *gloomy?*
   (a) somber   (b) drab   (c) obsolete   (d) hilarious

5. Which word or words go with *promise?*
   (a) vow   (b) dominate   (c) assume   (d) pledge

6. Which word or words go with *active?*
   (a) meager   (b) boisterous   (c) animated   (d) obsolete

7. Which word or words go with *persuade?*
   (a) betray   (b) convince   (c) retain   (d) provoke

8. Which word or words go with *become worse?*
   (a) decline   (b) negotiate   (c) deteriorate   (d) pardon

9. Which word or words go with *silly?*
   (a) obsolete   (b) somber   (c) absurd   (d) hilarious

10. Which word or words go with *out of date?*
    (a) animated   (b) obsolete   (c) hilarious   (d) mischievous

18c Determining Meanings

Circle the letter next to each answer choice that correctly completes the sentence. There may be more than one correct answer.

1. The **hilariously**
   (a) funny clown made us laugh till we cried.
   (b) missed goal meant they had lost the championship.
   (c) miserable illness affected several dozen people.
   (d) silly puppy tried to sleep on top of the ball.

2. **Somberly**
   (a) we told my dad about the hole we'd made in the fence.
   (b) we watched as the star quarterback was pulled from the game.
   (c) we decided not to go to the amusement park, because our dog was sick.
   (d) we jumped up and down when Zeniqua won the contest.

3. She **subsequently**
   (a) told a story that was the exact opposite of the story her friend had told.
   (b) found out that she could still join the volleyball team.
   (c) earned the money before she bought new clothes.
   (d) was able to balance the ball on her finger after lots of practice.

4. The **vows**
   (a) broke under the weight and had to be replaced.
   (b) they promised to each other were very serious.
   (c) were eaten quickly by the brothers.
   (d) to help the homeless were easy to make.

5. He **betrayed**
   (a) his friend's trust, which was unforgivable.
   (b) the newspapers and did the crossword puzzle.
   (c) down on the bed and tried to sleep.
   (d) how he really felt when he couldn't hide his smile.

animated

betray

convince

decline

hilarious

likeness

meager

mischief

negotiate

obsolete

retain

sensation

somber

subsequent

vow

6. The **sensation**
   (a) of falling and hitting the ground woke me from a deep sleep.
   (b) caused by the movie star's unexpected arrival would be on all the gossip websites tomorrow.
   (c) that something was wrong made me nervous.
   (d) to California was something I'd always wanted to do.

7. We **negotiated**
   (a) to make sure we were both happy.
   (b) with our rivals to see who would play first.
   (c) down the hill on the sled.
   (d) the water quickly because we were late and had to leave the pool.

8. The **mischievous**
   (a) shoelace got caught in the wheel, pulling her shoe off.
   (b) cup was on the bottom shelf.
   (c) pranks were so funny that we had to laugh.
   (d) giraffe leaned down and grabbed the man's hat.

18D Completing Sentences

Complete the sentences to demonstrate your knowledge of the words in bold.

1. One **vow** I have made to myself is

   _____.

2. A **sensational** vacation might be a trip to

   _____.

3. An example of a **meager** amount of food is

   _____.

4. Something a **mischievous** kitten might do is

   _____.

5. I am **convinced** that

   _____.

6. If you **retain** something, that means you

   _____.

7. I become **animated** whenever I

   _____.

8. When something becomes **obsolete,** that means it

   _____.

9. I become **somber** when

   _____.

10. A food I would **decline** is

   _____.

18E   Vocabulary in Context
Read the passage.

A Mouse Is Born

animated
betray
convince
decline
hilarious
likeness
meager
mischief
negotiate
obsolete
retain
sensation
somber
subsequent
vow

In 1927, Walt Disney worked in the movie business, producing short **animated** cartoons. He had started his own film company in Los Angeles four years before, at the age of twenty-one, with five hundred dollars borrowed from a relative. During those four years, his business provided him with a **meager** living; he worked hard on his films, struggling to pay off the debt.

His cartoons were about a character called Oswald, the Lucky Rabbit. A film distributor in New York had been buying his films and renting them to movie houses. The distributor could make a big profit if a film was successful. Disney, on the other hand, was paid a fixed amount for each movie; he got no share of the profits. When the contract with the distributor came to an end, Walt Disney decided to go to New York with his wife, Lilly, to **negotiate** a better deal for himself.

At the meeting, the distributor not only **declined** all of Disney's proposals, but also told the young filmmaker that he would reduce the payments he was making for each cartoon. He knew very well that Disney had no money to pay lawyers to fight him in the courts. Even worse, the distributor boasted that he had secretly hired Disney's own artists to do the drawings for future Oswald movies. Disney was bitter that the distributor had **betrayed** him, but there was nothing he could do about it. He **vowed** never to sell another of his movies to anyone. He would rent them to distributors, of course. In the future, though, he would **retain** ownership.

Walt Disney was in a **somber** mood when he and Lilly boarded the train for Los Angeles. During the long journey across the country, he decided to create a new character to take the place of Oswald. After making a few marks on paper, he showed Lilly a sketch of a mouse. Immediately she noticed the **likeness** between her husband and the creature he had drawn; both had a look of harmless **mischief.** She was **convinced** that audiences would love the little mouse with the happy face. She was dismayed, however, when her husband told her he planned to name it Mortimer. That just didn't sound right to her. "What about Mickey?" she suggested. "Mickey Mouse."

As soon as he arrived in Los Angeles, Walt Disney went to work on the first Mickey Mouse cartoons. He had completed two and was working on *Steamboat Willie*, his third, when sound began to be added to movies. Suddenly silent movies were **obsolete.** Disney promptly added a soundtrack to *Steamboat Willie*. The shrill voice of Mickey was supplied by Walt Disney himself.

When the movie opened in New York in September 1928, it was a **sensation.** Audiences roared with laughter at Mickey's **hilarious** adventures; **subsequent** movies starring the lovable little mouse were equally successful at the box office. In just three years Walt Disney's company was worth hundreds of thousands of dollars, and Mickey Mouse was famous.

▶ **Answer each of the following questions with a sentence. If a question does not contain a vocabulary word from the lesson's word list, use one in your answer. Use each word only once.**

1. How would you describe Walt Disney's income in 1927?

_____

_____

2. What work did Walt Disney do?

_____

_____

3. What is the meaning of **sensation** as it is used in the passage?

_____

_____

4. Why did Disney want to meet with the distributor?

_____

_____

5. Why didn't Disney get a lawyer and sue the New York distributor?

_____

_____

6. How did the distributor respond to Disney's proposals for a new contract?

_____

_____

7. What is the meaning of **betrayed** as it is used in the passage?

_____

_____

8. What **mischief** did the distributor boast of to Disney?

_____

_____

9. What is the meaning of **somber** as it is used in the passage?

_____

_____

10. What lesson did Disney learn from his experience with the distributor?

_____

_____

11. What did Lilly notice about the little mouse Walt Disney had drawn?

_____

_____

12. Why do you think silent movies became **obsolete?**

_____

_____

| animated |
| betray |
| convince |
| decline |
| hilarious |
| likeness |
| meager |
| mischief |
| negotiate |
| obsolete |
| retain |
| sensation |
| somber |
| subsequent |
| vow |

13. What did Lilly do when her husband suggested the name of Mortimer?

_____

_____

14. How many Disney movies, after *Steamboat Willie,* had sound?

_____

_____

15. Why did audiences enjoy *Steamboat Willie?*

_____

_____

Fun & Fascinating FACTS

- The Latin word for both "air" and "breath" is *anima*. It provides the root of several English words having to do with being alive, which seems natural because all *animals* must breathe in order to live. **Animated** figures in movie cartoons seem to be alive, while something that is *inanimate* lacks life. Stones, cars, coat hangers, and television sets are all *inanimate* objects.

- The adjective **somber** comes from the Latin word for "shade," which is *umbra*. Other words formed from this root include *umbrella,* which not only keeps off the rain but provides shade in bright sunlight, and *sombrero,* a Spanish or Mexican broad-brimmed hat worn to provide shade for the face.

convince

verb 1. To persuade.

2. To make someone feel more certain about something.

. . . .

Academic Context

When you write an opinion piece, you want to **convince** someone to agree with you. You provide facts and reasons to support your argument.

Context Clues

These sentences give clues to the meaning of **convinced.**

> Karolina **convinced** Josie to ride the roller coaster.

> Monty **convinced** his mother that he knew the way to the library by showing her the route on a map.

Discussion & Writing Prompt

Describe a time when someone **convinced** you to try something new.

2 min.	3 min.
1. Turn and talk to your partner or group.	**2.** Write 2–4 sentences.
Use this space to take notes or draw your ideas.	Be ready to share what you have written.

Study the definitions of the words. Then do the exercises that follow.

dormant
dôr´ mənt

adj. 1. In a sleeplike state.
Groundhogs remain **dormant** through the winter.

2. Not active, but able to become active.
Japan's Mount Fuji is a **dormant** volcano.

elegant
el´ ə gənt

adj. Graceful or refined in appearance or behavior.
The tiny curved numbers and the slender hands made the old silver watch an **elegant** timepiece.

erupt
ē rupt´

v. To burst forth violently.
The woman **erupted** in anger when she learned the store had just closed.

eruption *n.* A violent bursting forth.
The **eruption** of Mount Saint Helens in 1980 caused immense damage.

Show your partner how you can erupt in laughter.

excavate
eks´ kə vāt

v. 1. To dig out.
The backhoe will **excavate** this spot near the pine tree to create the basement of our new house.

2. To uncover by digging.
Workers began to **excavate** the ancient city of Troy in 1871.

excavation *n.* The place formed by digging or the process of digging out.
The **excavation** of Cahuachi, Peru, uncovered many pieces of pottery from the ancient Nazca culture.

Discuss with your partner a place near your school where workers could excavate to build a large swimming pool.

expel
ek spel´

v. 1. To eject; to release, as from a container.
Electric cars help keep the air clean because they don't **expel** poisonous gases.

2. To force to leave.
The school reserves the right to **expel** students for serious offenses.

Show your partner how you expel air from your lungs.

fume
fyo͞om

n. (usually plural) A disagreeable smoke or gas.
Fumes from passing trucks and buses have damaged the oak trees.

v. To feel or show anger or resentment.
My father **fumed** when he discovered that I had left my bicycle out in the rain all night.

molten
mōlt´n

adj. Made liquid by heat; melted.
At the craft fair, we watched people make tapers by dipping wicks into pots of **molten** wax.

painstaking
pānz´tāk iŋ

adj. Showing or taking great care or effort.
After a **painstaking** search of the house, we found the missing car keys.

perish
per´ish

v. To die; to be killed or destroyed.
Approximately ten million people **perished** in World War I.

population
păp yo͞o lā´shən

n. 1. The total number of people in a certain place.
The **population** of the town declined by almost a quarter over the past decade.

2. The total number of plants or animals in a certain area.
The elm tree **population** decreased greatly after the 1930s because of Dutch elm disease.

populate *v.* To fill; to form the population of.
I wish I had as many adventures as the characters who **populate** my favorite book.

Chat with your partner about what animals in your area have the highest populations.

prelude
prel´yo͞od

n. 1. Something that comes before or introduces the main part.
The October frost was a **prelude** to a harsh winter.

2. A short musical piece played as an introduction.
Chang-lee played a piano **prelude** for the spring recital.

Tell your partner the name of the meal that is a prelude to lunch.

scald
skôld

v. To burn with hot liquid or steam.
Boiling water from the overturned saucepan **scalded** the man's hand.

scalding *adj.* Very hot.
The bath water was **scalding,** so I added some cold water.

stupendous
stoo pen´ dəs

adj. Amazing because it is very great or very large.
It took a **stupendous** effort to return the beached whales to the water.

Discuss with your partner something there is stupendous number of, such as stars in the sky.

suffocate
suf´ ə kāt

v. To kill or die by stopping access to air.
The trapped miners **suffocated** when their air supply was cut off.

suffocation *n.* The act or process of suffocating.
Keep plastic bags away from young children to avoid any chance of **suffocation.**

Talk with your partner about what to do if someone is suffocating.

tremor
trem´ ər

n. 1. A shaking movement.
Tremors following the 1994 Los Angeles earthquake continued for several weeks.

2. A nervous or excited feeling.
When I heard the front door creak open, a **tremor** of fear ran through me.

19A Finding Meanings

Choose two phrases to form a sentence that correctly uses a word from Word List 19. Then write the sentence.

1. (a) forbid people to go into it.
   (b) fill it with people.
   (c) To populate an area is to
   (d) To excavate an area is to

   _____

   _____

2. (a) To perish
   (b) is to tire easily.
   (c) To fume
   (d) is to die.

   _____

   _____

3. (a) break up into smaller parts.   (c) To suffocate is to
   (b) burst out violently.   (d) To erupt is to

   _____

   _____

4. (a) An excavated building is one   (c) that is beautifully designed.
   (b) An elegant building is one   (d) that has been completely rebuilt.

   _____

   _____

5. (a) that is amazingly large.   (c) A stupendous job is one
   (b) A painstaking job is one   (d) that is very boring.

   _____

   _____

6. (a) To scald is   (c) to burn with a hot liquid.
   (b) To expel is   (d) to taunt.

   _____

   _____

7. (a) To be painstaking is to   (c) take very great care.
   (b) be careless of others' feelings.   (d) To be dormant is to

   _____

   _____

8. (a) be prevented from getting air.   (c) To erupt is to
   (b) be permitted to enter.   (d) To suffocate is to

   _____

   _____

9. (a) Something that is molten is   (c) made liquid by heat.
   (b) easily damaged.   (d) Something that is dormant is

   _____

   _____

10. (a) Fumes are   (c) harmful gases.
    (b) Tremors are   (d) burns caused by hot liquids.

    _____

    _____

dormant
elegant
erupt
excavate
expel
fume
molten
painstaking
perish
population
prelude
scald
stupendous
suffocate
tremor

Just the Right Word

Replace each phrase in bold with a single word (or form of the word) from the word list.

1. In the hot, crowded room, he felt like he was **unable to breathe.**

2. When the pipe broke, there was a sudden **bursting out** of steam.

3. The **total number of people living** in the city of New York is over eight million.

4. Some of the passengers began to **feel very angry** when they were told the train would be an hour late.

5. Chopin made people appreciate the **short musical piece played as an introduction.**

6. The maple trees that line the driveway are **in an inactive state with no signs of life** during the winter.

7. Parkinson's disease causes **rapid back-and-forth shaking movements** in the hands.

8. The Martian volcano known as Olympus Mons is **amazing because of its great size.**

9. The **process of digging a hole in the ground** revealed the remains of an ancient Chinese temple.

10. The school suspended the minor offenders, but those guilty of major offenses were **forced to leave for good.**

19c Applying Meanings

Circle the letter or letters next to each correct answer. There may be more than one correct answer.

1. Which of the following could be **excavated?**
   - (a) smoke
   - (b) a secret
   - (c) soil
   - (d) a buried city

2. Which of the following can be **dormant?**
   - (a) a volcano
   - (b) a rock
   - (c) a tree
   - (d) an animal

3. Which of the following can **scald** someone?
   - (a) a hot beverage
   - (b) a hot iron
   - (c) a hot temper
   - (d) a hot day

4. Which of the following could be **elegant?**
   - (a) an aroma
   - (b) a restaurant
   - (c) a meal
   - (d) a dress

5. Which of the following can **perish?**
   - (a) people
   - (b) time
   - (c) hope
   - (d) freedom

6. Which of the following can cause **tremors?**
   - (a) a sickness
   - (b) an earthquake
   - (c) excitement
   - (d) fear

7. Which of the following can **erupt?**
   - (a) an excited crowd
   - (b) a riot
   - (c) an active volcano
   - (d) an angry character

8. Which of the following can give off **fumes?**
   - (a) a faulty oil furnace
   - (b) a car's exhaust
   - (c) an angry person
   - (d) a lighted oil lamp

dormant
elegant
erupt
excavate
expel
fume
molten
painstaking
perish
population
prelude
scald
stupendous
suffocate
tremor

19D Word Study: Prefixes

Complete each sentence with a word from this list.

exult	excavate	expel	extract	extinct
export	expand	experiment	exasperate	exhale

1. To _____ cream from milk is to take the cream out.

2. To _____ is to cry out for joy.

3. To become _____ is to die out completely.

4. To _____ is to try something out to see if it works.

5. To _____ something is to send it out of the country.

6. To _____ is to spread out.

7. To _____ someone is to force that person out.

8. To _____ something is to dig it out of the ground.

9. To _____ someone is to wear out that person's patience.

10. To _____ is to breathe out.

19E Vocabulary in Context

Read the passage.

The Lost City

Two thousand years ago, Pompeii was a prosperous town with a **population** of perhaps twenty thousand people. It was a busy port located on the Sarnus River, near the Bay of Naples. That is about 130 miles south of Rome. Rich landowners and retired Roman citizens built **elegant** homes in the town and paid for its fine public buildings and temples. The town was nestled in the shadow of four-thousand-foot-high Mount Vesuvius. Local farmers cultivated grapes in the mountainside's fertile soil as they had done for centuries.

In 62 CE, the town was shaken by **tremors** from an earthquake; for the next seventeen years, the people worked to repair the damage. They were not then aware of the danger they were in. If they had known what we know today, that earthquake would have been a warning to them. **Stupendous** forces were slowly building deep beneath the surface; the earthquake was merely the **prelude** to a far worse disaster.

Mount Vesuvius is a volcano. It had been **dormant** for eight hundred years; there had been no activity during this time. That was because a thick layer of **molten** rock, called lava, had hardened to form a plug, sealing off the mouth of the volcano like a cork in a bottle. Over the centuries, pressure deep below the earth's surface had been slowly building up inside the volcano. On August 24, 79 CE, it became so great that the plug of lava was suddenly **expelled** in a tremendous explosion.

So violent was the explosion that the top of the mountain was blown off. Cracks appeared in the earth. Water, heated to boiling by fires beneath the earth's crust, thrust its way to the surface. People and animals were **scalded** as they tried to flee. Smoke, poisonous **fumes,** and ash from the volcano filled the air, **suffocating** many people in their homes. Buildings were crushed by huge rocks hurled from the volcano. Then came a series of avalanches that buried the town, together with everything in it, in twenty feet of stones, cinders, and volcanic ash.

A vivid description of the **eruption** of Vesuvius was given by Pliny the Younger, who later became a famous Roman statesman. He was eighteen years old at the time. Pliny the Younger watched the disaster from twenty miles away on the other side of the bay. His uncle sailed to Pompeii to save the lives of some friends but died during the attempt. Pliny the Younger described the tragic events of that day in letters he wrote many years later.

For centuries Pompeii lay buried and forgotten. It was not until 1763 that the **excavation** of the ruins first began. **Painstaking** digging revealed streets and buildings filled with the objects of everyday life. Also uncovered were the bodies of the more than two thousand people who **perished** on that terrible day nearly two thousand years ago when the sleeping volcano suddenly woke up.

dormant
elegant
erupt
excavate
expel
fume
molten
painstaking
perish
population
prelude
scald
stupendous
suffocate
tremor

▶ **Answer each of the following questions with a sentence. If a question does not contain a vocabulary word from the lesson's word list, use one in your answer. Use each word only once.**

1. What did the **excavations** at Pompeii reveal?

   _____

   _____

2. Why were the citizens of Pompeii unconcerned about Mount Vesuvius?

   _____

   _____

3. What is the meaning of **prelude** as it is used in the passage?

   _____

   _____

4. What evidence is there that some of Pompeii's people were wealthy?

   _____

   _____

5. What is the meaning of **tremors** as it is used in the passage?

   _____

   _____

6. What happened when the pressure inside the volcano became too great?

   _____

   _____

7. Why did the explosion of Vesuvius have such **stupendous** force?

   _____

   _____

8. What are some materials that were thrust from the volcano when it exploded?

   _____

   _____

9. What is the meaning of **expelled** as it is used in the passage?

   _____

   _____

10. Why do you think uncovering Pompeii was such **painstaking** work?

_____

_____

11. Why did the underground water from Vesuvius cause deaths and injuries?

_____

_____

12. Why was the air at Pompeii dangerous to breathe?

_____

_____

13. What happened to Pliny the Younger's uncle?

_____

_____

14. How many people lived in Pompeii?

_____

_____

15. What were the three major causes of death at Pompeii?

_____

_____

dormant
elegant
erupt
excavate
expel
fume
molten
painstaking
perish
population
prelude
scald
stupendous
suffocate
tremor

Fun & Fascinating FACTS

- The dormouse is a European animal resembling a small squirrel. It hibernates in winter. This sleeplike state is what gives it its name: the Latin for "sleep" is *dormire.* Other English words formed from this Latin word are **dormant** and *dormitory,* a place where people sleep.

- The noun and adjective *perishable* are formed from the verb **perish.** *Perishable* foods spoil quickly, and *perishables* are any foods, such as tomatoes and lettuce, that spoil quickly.

- What do *premature* (Word List 3), *previous* (Word List 5), *predict* (Word List 15), and **prelude** all have in common? All four are formed from the Latin prefix *pre-,* which means "before." And notice where a *prefix* is found. It comes *before* the rest of the word.

expel

verb 1. To release from a container.

2. To force to leave.

Word Family
expelled (verb)
expulsion (noun)

Word Parts
The prefix *ex-* often means "out" or "away."
Other words with this prefix are *excavate* and *exhale*. What are some other words with the prefix *ex-?*

Discussion & Writing Prompt

*When the car sped away, it **expelled** a thick cloud of black smoke.*

Based on this sentence, write the definition of **expelled** and then use it in a new sentence of your own.

2 min.	**3 min.**
1. Turn and talk to your partner or group.	**2.** Write 2–4 sentences.
Use this space to take notes or draw your ideas.	Be ready to share what you have written.

Study the definitions of the words. Then do the exercises that follow.

ample
am´ pəl

adj. 1. Plenty; more than enough.
One large turkey will provide **ample** food for eight people.

2. Large in size.
The cat's **ample** stomach was proof that he was given plenty of food.

burden
bʊrd´ n

n. 1. Something that is carried, especially a heavy load.
Carrying his frail son on his shoulder was never a **burden.**

2. Anything that is hard to bear.
The **burden** of caring for four sick children was too much for the babysitter.

v. To add to what one has to bear.
Don't **burden** your grandparents with this problem.

Discuss with your partner how you could help a friend who has a large burden of chores.

compassion
kəm pash´ ən

n. A feeling of sharing the suffering of others and of wanting to help; sympathy; pity.
Shazia's **compassion** for the homeless led to her working each weekend at the soup kitchen.

compassionate *adj.* The state of showing compassion.
The doctor's **compassionate** manner made her loved by all of her patients.

Tell your partner how a compassionate friend or family member has helped you.

comply
kəm plī´

v. To act in agreement with a rule or another's wishes.
Unless you **comply** with the requirement to wear shoes, you cannot enter the restaurant.

cumbersome
kum´ bər səm

adj. Awkward and hard to handle; unwieldy.
The crate of oranges was **cumbersome,** but the clerk managed to get it up the stairs.

distress
di stres´

v. To cause pain or sorrow; to trouble or worry.
It **distresses** me that no one offered to help when they saw the accident.

n. Pain, sorrow, or worry.
Our class felt **distress** because of our friend's illness, so we made a large poster with our get-well wishes.

encounter
en koun´ tər

v. 1. To meet unexpectedly.
The actress **encountered** a crowd of fans in the lobby of her hotel.

2. To be faced with.
As the frightened children ran around the corner, they **encountered** a stone wall.

n. 1. A chance meeting.
Our **encounter** with our neighbors at the party was a pleasant surprise.

2. A battle or fight.
The first major **encounter** of the Civil War occurred at Fort Sumter on April 12, 1861.

Show your partner what happens if a pen or pencil encounters a piece of scrap paper.

---

exert
eg zʉrt´

v. To put forth effort.
If Jane doesn't **exert** herself more in Spanish class, I'm sure she will not be able to speak the language.

exertion *n.* The act of tiring oneself; a strong effort.
The **exertion** of climbing to the top of the ruins left the explorers feeling weak.

Show your partner what you would look like if you were tired from exertion.

---

indignant
in dig´ nənt

adj. Angry or resentful about something that seems wrong or unfair.
Brandisha was **indignant** when her friend ignored her repeated texts.

indignation *n.* Anger that is caused by something mean or unfair.
My **indignation** was aroused when I was not given a chance to defend myself.

Discuss with your partner what to do if someone becomes indignant while playing a friendly game with you.

---

jest
jest

n. A joke or the act of joking.
My remark was made in **jest;** I'm sorry you took me seriously.

v. To joke or say things lightheartedly.
"Surely you **jest,**" I said when my aunt suggested throwing out the television set.

---

mirth
mʉrth

n. Laughter; joyfulness expressed through laughter.
The sight of the three-year-old wearing her mother's hat and shoes provoked much **mirth** among the family.

moral
môr´ əl

n. A useful lesson about life.
The play's **moral** was "Look before you leap."

adj. 1. Having to do with questions of right and wrong.
Animal cruelty is a **moral** as well as a legal issue.

2. Based on what is right and proper.
You have a **moral** duty to report a crime if you see it.

Tell your partner whom you talk to when you are faced with a moral decision.

outskirts
out´ skʉrts

n. The parts far from the center, as of a town.
The plan to build another large shopping mall on the **outskirts** of town was voted down at the meeting.

resume
re zo͞om´

v. 1. To begin again after a pause.
The concert will **resume** after a fifteen-minute break.

2. To occupy again.
After the quick stop, the bus passengers **resumed** their seats for the next part of the journey.

Sit silently for fifteen seconds and then resume your work on this lesson.

ridicule
rid´ i kyo͞ol

v. To make fun of; to mock.
People once **ridiculed** the idea that flight by heavier-than-air machines was possible.

n. Words or actions intended to make fun of or mock.
Their **ridicule** of my friend finally provoked me to lose my temper.

ridiculous *adj.* Laughable; deserving of mockery.
It is **ridiculous** to suggest that a bridge could be built across the Atlantic Ocean.

20Ⓐ Using Words in Context

Read the following sentences. If the word in bold is used correctly, write C on the line. If the word is used incorrectly, write I on the line.

1. (a) Being poor was never really a **burden** for my family. _____
   (b) The **burden** was heavy, but no one complained. _____
   (c) Candace doesn't like to **burden** her friends with all her troubles. _____
   (d) A bowl of **burden** is very refreshing on a hot day. _____

2. (a) The students show their **compassion** by volunteering at the animal shelter. ____

   (b) Alejandro is studying acting and feels **compassionately** about the theater. ____

   (c) The **compassion** of a light bulb causes it to heat up. ____

   (d) A **compassionate** note of kindness was given to the victims. ____

3. (a) The large chair was too **cumbersome** for us to carry easily. ____

   (b) She smiled and gave me a **cumbersome** look as she skipped out the door. ____

   (c) Checking out all these books from the library will be **cumbersome,** but I need them. ____

   (d) Sunshine shone in **cumbersome** beams on the neighborhood. ____

4. (a) We **encountered** a few bumps on our trip. ____

   (b) The **encounter** ended when the dog ran away and the cat purred. ____

   (c) I **encountered** an old friend when I returned to my hometown. ____

   (d) I **encountered** how many eggs we have, but I forget the number. ____

5. (a) The coach **exerted** that he was sure they would win the game. ____

   (b) You must **exert** pressure on the handle to release the brake. ____

   (c) The **exertion** of running all the way home made me so tired. ____

   (d) **Exert** the book back to me when you're done reading it. ____

6. (a) The **jest** was funny enough to make some of us laugh. ____

   (b) I was speaking in **jest** when I said I was quitting the team. ____

   (c) Don't **jest** about something as serious as your safety! ____

   (d) Keep the good ones and throw the **jest** away. ____

7. (a) **Mirth** was piled up in the driveway. ____

   (b) My brother tried to hide his **mirth** when I saw what he did to my room. ____

   (c) The **mirth** in the car grew louder as more of us got the joke. ____

   (d) He tried to tell us that the **mirth** wasn't ready yet. ____

8. (a) The **moral** of the story is "Always tell the truth." ____

   (b) The **moral** thing to do is to return the money you found. ____

   (c) The **moral** we caught was at least three feet long. ____

   (d) The **moral** ended happily with the friends reunited. ____

9. (a) I **resumed** that you would be coming with us. _____
   (b) The campers **resumed** all the food that we brought with us. _____
   (c) The play **resumed** after the actor stopped coughing. _____
   (d) Mrs. Muhammad **resumed** teaching after she had her baby. _____

10. (a) The suggestion was met with **ridicule** by the class. _____
    (b) It's **ridiculous** to suggest that I could climb Mount Everest. _____
    (c) We got rid of the **ridicule** but managed to save the good stuff. _____
    (d) The **ridicule** was harvested in the spring by the farmers. _____

20B Making Connections

Circle the letter next to each correct answer. There may be more than one correct answer.

1. Which word or words go with *feeling bad?*
   (a) humiliated   (b) distress   (c) precious   (d) forlorn

2. Which word or words go with *feeling angry?*
   (a) compassion   (b) indignation   (c) ridicule   (d) outrage

3. Which word or words go with *not in the city?*
   (a) outskirts   (b) urban   (c) moral   (d) jubilee

4. Which word or words go with *make fun of?*
   (a) negotiate   (b) mimic   (c) mock   (d) ridicule

5. Which word or words go with *sympathy?*
   (a) ample   (b) artificial   (c) somber   (d) compassionate

6. Which word or words go with *begin again?*
   (a) resume   (b) comply   (c) encounter   (d) decline

7. Which word or words go with *clumsy?*
   (a) indignant   (b) unwieldy   (c) cumbersome   (d) hilarious

| ample |
| burden |
| compassion |
| comply |
| cumbersome |
| distress |
| encounter |
| exert |
| indignant |
| jest |
| mirth |
| moral |
| outskirts |
| resume |
| ridicule |

8. Which word or words go with *joke?*
   (a) vow   (b) jest   (c) prank   (d) likeness

9. Which word or words go with *agree to do something?*
   (a) decline   (b) resume   (c) encounter   (d) comply

10. Which word or words go with *enough?*
   (a) sufficient   (b) indignant
   (c) compassionate   (d) ample

20C Determining Meanings

Circle the letter next to each answer choice that correctly completes the sentence. There may be more than one correct answer.

1. The **burdensome**
   (a) salad was eaten as soon as it was ready.
   (b) table was too heavy for one person.
   (c) road is always clear and easy for my mom to drive on.
   (d) lie was all I could think about.

2. I was **distressed**
   (a) to read that everything was going to be OK.
   (b) into my seat on the giant roller coaster.
   (c) by reports that the park might close for good.
   (d) to hear about your injured dog.

3. The **jesting**
   (a) began, but I knew they weren't serious.
   (b) made Usma laugh harder and harder.
   (c) kept getting bigger and bigger until it exploded.
   (d) on the lake swirled in the early morning light.

4. The **outskirts**
   (a) kept billowing in the wind until we tied them down.
   (b) of the town seemed the right place to have a bike race.
   (c) of the thunder crashed three times in a row.
   (d) had only a few houses but mostly trees.

5. The **ridiculousness**

    (a) of the movie was obvious.

    (b) should be eaten in small amounts.

    (c) in the tissues are at the bottom of the stairs.

    (d) was almost too funny to ignore.

6. She was **mirthless**

    (a) because she hadn't had much sleep.

    (b) as she hopped up and down with excitement.

    (c) about the difficult test that was coming up.

    (d) but said she would try to get in a good mood.

7. Paulo **encountered**

    (a) the ants on the bed and yelled.

    (b) all of us in his family's kitchen for the surprise party.

    (c) how many chairs he would need.

    (d) off the diving board into the pool.

8. The **exertion**

    (a) on the sign told us not to go any farther.

    (b) during the first day of practice made us more tired than we expected.

    (c) was through the door at the end of the hall.

    (d) of playing two soccer games in a row will be intense.

ample
burden
compassion
comply
cumbersome
distress
encounter
exert
indignant
jest
mirth
moral
outskirts
resume
ridicule

Complete the sentences to demonstrate your knowledge of the words in bold.

1. If you **ridicule** something, that means you

    _____.

2. I would feel **indignant** if

    _____.

3. An example of something a **moral** person would do is

    _____.

4. I **exerted** myself today when I

    _____.

5. When you **comply** with a rule, that means you

    _____.

6. Someone from history that I wish I could have an **encounter** with is

    _____.

7. Something that would **distress** me about school is

    _____.

8. One way to show you feel **compassion** for someone is to

    _____.

9. Something that would be a **burden** to carry is

    _____.

10. If you look full of **mirth,** that means

    _____.

A Tale of Two Donkeys

Aesop was an enslaved person who lived in ancient Greece. Although little is known about his life, readers have enjoyed the fables he told for more than twenty-five centuries. Not only are his stories entertaining, but they also teach us something about human behavior, for a fable is a story with a lesson. The characters in them can be animals who talk and behave like humans, or they can be ordinary people, like those in the story that follows.

A farmer and his daughter were on their way to market to sell a donkey. The farmer rode on the animal's back while the daughter plodded along at his side. After they had gone about a mile, they happened to **encounter** a woman drawing water from a well. She was very **indignant** at the sight of the farmer riding in ease while his daughter had to walk. She told the farmer that he should be ashamed of himself. So, to please her, the father and daughter changed places. When the young woman was sitting comfortably on the donkey, they **resumed** their journey.

Just as they reached the **outskirts** of the town, they met a young man. He asked the farmer why he was walking when there was **ample** room for both of them on the donkey. To please the young man, the farmer climbed onto the donkey behind his daughter and they continued on their way.

A little later they passed by two women standing by the side of the road. When they saw the donkey carrying two grown people, the women were filled with **compassion** for the animal. "Have you any idea of the **distress** you are causing that poor donkey?" the older woman called out to the farmer. "The poor creature is half dead from having to carry such a **burden**." The younger woman loudly remarked that the farmer and his daughter should be carrying the donkey instead of the donkey carrying them. She spoke in **jest.** The farmer, however, took her seriously and at once set about to **comply** with her suggestion.

First, he tied the donkey's legs to a pole. This took some time, as the donkey had no desire to have its legs tied, but at last the task was accomplished. Such a **cumbersome** load was difficult for the farmer and his daughter to lift. But finally, they managed to hoist the pole onto their shoulders. With the donkey slung upside down between them and struggling to escape, they staggered down the road.

ample
burden
compassion
comply
cumbersome
distress
encounter
exert
indignant
jest
mirth
moral
outskirts
resume
ridicule

At last, panting from their **exertions,** they reached the market. Their arrival was greeted with considerable **mirth,** so that when the farmer tried to sell the donkey, his attempts were **ridiculed.** For, of course, no one was willing to buy a donkey that had to be carried.

Can you guess the **moral** of this fable? The Hidden Message puzzle in the review section at the end of this lesson will spell it out for you.

▶ **Answer each of the following questions with a sentence. If a question does not contain a vocabulary word from the lesson's word list, use one in your answer. Use each word only once.**

1. How do you think people responded when Aesop told this story?

_____

_____

2. How do you think the ending of the story would have changed if the farmer and his daughter had not **encountered** anyone on the way to town?

_____

_____

3. What reason do you think Aesop had for telling this story?

_____

_____

4. Why might one feel **compassion** for the farmer's daughter?

_____

_____

5. Why do you think the farmer never became **indignant** when people kept telling him what to do?

_____

_____

6. How did the farmer respond to the various suggestions that were made?

_____

_____

7. What is the meaning of **burden** as it is used in the passage?

_____

_____

8. In what way did the farmer misunderstand the young woman who suggested that he and his daughter should carry the donkey?

_____

_____

9. What do you think probably **distressed** the donkey most?

_____

_____

10. Why would it be difficult for two people to carry a donkey?

_____

_____

11. What is the meaning of **resumed** as it is used in the passage?

_____

_____

12. How does the passage make clear that the farmer and his daughter found carrying the donkey hard work?

_____

_____

13. What is the meaning of **ample** as it is used in the passage?

_____

_____

14. Where were the farmer and his daughter when they met the young man?

_____

_____

15. How do you think the farmer and his daughter must have looked when they reached the market?

_____

_____

ample
burden
compassion
comply
cumbersome
distress
encounter
exert
indignant
jest
mirth
moral
outskirts
resume
ridicule

Fun & Fascinating FACTS

- The Greek word *pathos,* which means "suffering," has passed unchanged into English via Latin. It means "something that moves a person to feel pity." By combining the Latin root with the prefix *con* (also written *com-* or *col-*), which means "with" or "together," we form the word **compassion.** Several other words are formed from this root. *Sympathy* has the same meaning as *compassion,* although the latter term suggests a greater depth of feeling. *Pathetic* means "arousing feelings of pity." (The *pathetic* cries of the injured animal moved us to tears.)

- The language spoken in France from the ninth to the early sixteenth century is called Old French. The Old French verb *encombrer* meant "to put obstacles in the way of." **Cumbersome** and several other English words have been formed from this Old French verb. To *encumber* someone is to put a heavy load on that person. (Hikers who are *encumbered* with heavy backpacks are glad of a chance to rest.) An *encumbrance* is anything that is awkward, difficult, or heavy. (Heavy boots are an *encumbrance* when running to catch a school bus.)

- **Resume** is a noun meaning "a brief outline or summary, especially of a person's education and work experience." It is sometimes written with a stroke, or accent, over each *e: résumé.* This is done because it is the French spelling, and *resume* is a French word brought into English. With this meaning, the word is pronounced the French way, *REZ-oo-may.*

Vocabulary Extension

encounter

verb 1. To meet, often without expecting to.

2. To experience a problem.

noun An unexpected meeting.

Context Clues

These sentences give clues to the meaning of **encounter.**

> *The dogs growled when they **encountered** each other at the park.*
>
> *Camila's work was interrupted when she **encountered** a computer error.*
>
> *Nihar was excited to tell us about an accidental **encounter** with his favorite soccer player.*

Discussion & Writing Prompt

Write about the different people you might **encounter** at a school sports game.

2 min.

1. Turn and talk to your partner or group.

Use this space to take notes or draw your ideas.

3 min.

2. Write 2–4 sentences.

Be ready to share what you have written.

_____

_____

_____

_____

_____

_____

_____

_____

_____

_____

_____

_____

Lessons 17–20

Review

Hidden Message   In the spaces provided to the right of each sentence, write the vocabulary words from Lessons 17 through 20 that are missing in each of the sentences. Be sure that the words you choose fit the meaning of each sentence and have the same number of letters as there are spaces. The number after each sentence is the lesson the word is from. If the exercise is done correctly, the shaded boxes will spell out the moral of Aesop's fable from Lesson 20.

1. Plants _____ if they are not watered. (17)

2. I warned the child not to get into any _____. (18)

3. All _____ meetings went better than the first one. (18)

4. I will _____ my journey in the morning. (20)

5. The waves are starting to _____ the cliff. (17)

6. It would _____ me to see you hurt in any way. (20)

7. I was filled with _____ for the homeless people. (20)

8. The _____ of China is over one billion. (19)

9. These _____ tools are ten thousand years old. (17)

10. I had an odd _____ as though I were being watched. (18)

11. I made a(n) _____ that I would never give up. (18)

12. A(n) _____ avalanche almost buried the village. (19)

13. Some plants stay _____ over the winter. (19)

14. I was afraid that the smoke would _____ me. (19)

15. The first flowers are a(n) _____ to spring. (19)

16. We made a(n) _____ search of the building. (19)

17. Don't _____ yourself if you're feeling tired. (20)

18. I tried not to _____ my true feelings. (18)

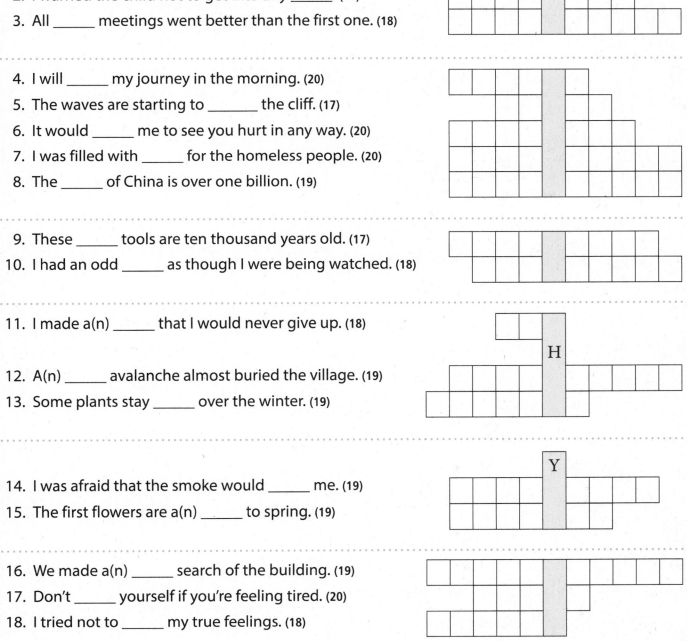

r uncle _____ ownership of the house? **(18)**

ı _____ any problems with the project? **(20)**

ı is used to _____ hot air from the kitchen. **(19)**

ust _____ your kind offer. **(18)**

.glected gardens soon _____ to weeds. **(17)**

ne comic's _____ jokes made the crowd roar. **(18)**

Our new house is on the _____ of town. **(20)**

The oak desk was a(n) _____ piece of furniture. **(20)**

7. The _____ glass glowed a bright cherry red. **(19)**

28. What will you do with the soil that you _____? **(19)**

29. The disease causes a(n) _____ in the patient's hands. **(19)**

30. _____ soil produces good crops. **(17)**

31. A(n) _____ in the Sahara is a welcome sight. **(17)**

32. Taking a deep breath will _____ your chest. **(17)**

33. He began to _____ at the long delay. **(19)**

34. Will you _____ with my request? **(20)**

35. We hope to _____ an end to the feud. **(18)**

36. Don't _____ those who are different from you. **(20)**

37. The graduation party was in a(n) _____ hotel. **(19)**

38. When crops fail, the result is often _____. **(17)**

39. I set down my _____ and rested a while. **(20)**

40. The long _____ ended with a heavy rainstorm. **(17)**

41. We have _____ time to make it to the bus station. **(20)**

42. Desert areas are mostly _____ and little grows there. (17)

43. He's liable to _____ in anger without any reason. (19)

44. Blindness did not _____ her until she was 70. (17)

45. They will _____ if they are not rescued soon. (19)

46. The small apple was a(n) _____ meal. (18)

47. This field provides good _____ for the horses. (17)

48. My clown costume caused a lot of _____. (20)

49. Do you see a(n) _____ between my cousin and me? (18)

50. We found _____ from the storm in an old hut. (17)

51. How can I _____ you I am telling the truth? (18)

52. The wide-spread use of electricity made gas lamps _____. (18)

53. The funeral put us all in a(n) _____ mood. (18)

54. I was _____ when I was told I had been left out. (20)

55. Please don't _____ about such a serious thing. (20)

Pronunciation Key

Symbol	Key Words	Symbol	Key Words
a	cat	b	bed
ā	ape	d	dog
ä	cot, car	f	fall
â	bear	g	get
		h	help
e	ten, berry	j	jump
ē	me	k	kiss, call
		l	leg, bottle
i	fit	m	meat
ī	ice, fire	n	nose, kitten
		p	put
ō	go	r	red
ô	fall, for	s	see
oi	oil	t	top
o͞o	look, pull	v	vat
o͞o	tool, rule	w	wish
ou	out, crowd	y	yard
		z	zebra
u	up		
ʉ	fur, shirt	ch	chin, arch
		ŋ	ring, drink
ə	a in ago	sh	she, push
	e in agent	th	thin, truth
	i in pencil	th	then, father
	o in atom	zh	measure
	u in circus		

A stress mark ´ is placed after a syllable that gets a primary stress, as in **vocabulary** (vō kab´ yə ler ē).